Sharing the Vision

Also by Lavinia Byrne

Women before God

Sharing the Vision

The Spiritual Lessons of the Religious Life

Lavinia Byrne

1989
COWLEY PUBLICATIONS
Cambridge, Massachusetts

Published in the United States of America by Cowley
Publications, a division of the Society of St. John the
Evangelist. Without limiting the rights under copyright
reserved above, no portion of this book may be
reproduced, stored in or introduced into a retrieval system,
or transmitted, in any form or by any means (electronic,
mechanical, photocopying, recording or otherwise,)
without the prior written permission of Cowley
Publications, except in the case of brief quotations
embodied in critical articles and reviews.

International Standard Book Number: 0-936384-80-8

The front cover illustration is reproduced by courtesy of
the Institutshaus Augsburg.

Library of Congress Cataloging-in-Publications Data
Byrne, Lavinia, 1947 –
　　Sharing the Vision : the spiritual lessons of the religious
life / Lavinia Byrne
　　　　p. cm.
　　Includes bibliographical references.
　　ISBN 0-936384-80-8 : $7.95
　　1. Monastic and religious life of woman. 2. Christian
life—Catholic authors. 3. Byrne, Lavinia, 1947 – . I. Title.
BX4210.B97 1989
255—dc20   89-22143

This book is printed on acid-free paper and was produced
in the United States of America.

Cowley Publications
980 Memorial Drive
Cambridge, Massachusetts 02138

To P. P. who encouraged me by writing:

'I am glad we are not bishops. If we were, how could we relate to all the confusing and ambiguous signals as real people, as part of the struggle? You are tapping a pure vein at the interface of faith and experience with tradition and you are laying it out with great clarity — *and* love, which is so important. I think we should be glad to be where we are, even though it is hard sometimes.'

Contents

Introduction   1

1   Images of religious life   5

2   Into the desert   14

3   Onto the mountain   24

4   The valley and beyond   33

5   Reclaiming the market place   42

6   Contemplating the universe   51

7   The place of the home   60

8   A context for holding: chastity   69

9   A context for owning: poverty   79

10   A context for choosing: obedience   88

Afterword   99

Books referred to in the text   101

Introduction

A year ago I was asked to teach a group of novices from a variety of religious congregations about the history of the religious life. To my alarm I later discovered that the novice masters and mistresses who were in charge of the first formation of the women and men in question were also to be among the group of fifty I would have to address. The bicycle ride down to Chelsea did nothing to allay my fears; it just confirmed my suspicion that what I was attempting to do was arrogant. I come from one tradition and have a certain understanding of what it means and what its demands may be. How could I presume to interpret other traditions?

Later one of the novices in question came to me for spiritual direction. Over a period of time she decided that she would leave the congregation which she had entered. At her final session at the novices' training course she told some of her contemporaries about her decision. Some of them registered a reaction which fascinated me. 'Why', they asked, 'have you come back to follow the course? Why are you still with us?' Their reaction acted on me as a catalyst and I found myself saying, 'If the course isn't good enough for people who are planning to live a lay life, how can it be any good to people who are planning to live the religious life?'

Both what we do and why we do it need constant commentary and explanation. Every vision given to the Church through the experience of Christian women and men down the ages can usefully be analysed and commented upon because in this way it yields up its treasures to the present. Only in this way can the visions of the past be shared in the present and informed by the present. Who should best do the commenting is of course an open question. Maybe it does have to be an outsider. Certainly I was

1

ignorant when I first set off to share ideas and listen to the
comments of people in religious formation — both on the giving
and the receiving end — but perhaps I was not as arrogant as I
first feared.

There are certain questions we can all afford to hear. Those I
found myself addressing to the religious life were: 'What?', 'Why?'
and 'How?' Moreover as I reflected on these questions I came to
see that the answers I was furnishing had a wider application.
Later these were commented on in the assessment the novices
were asked to submit at the end of the course. Two other factors
stirred my imagination. These were trends I observe when I look
at the way in which Christian women and men are attempting to
live and make sense of the idea of vocation in today's Church and
today's world. There is an acute shortage of vocations to the
religious life as traditionally conceived while there is a real
richness in the generosity with which lay people are living
committed Christian lives in the world. These are not two separate
comments. They belong together inescapably and pose real
questions about how the relationship of lay people and religious
may be mutually beneficial. The other factor which has haunted
my understanding over the last few years is that Esther de Waal's
book *Seeking God* has spoken to more people about both the
wisdom of traditional Benedictine life and its applications to
present-day living than most books written by Benedictines. As
an Anglican lay woman she might not have appeared to some
people to be the most obvious commentator on the Rule of St
Benedict. As it happened her experience as a homemaker and as
wife of the Dean of Canterbury brought real authority to her
insights into the Rule. So too with Grace Jantzen's *Julian of
Norwich* and Margaret Hebblethwaite's *Seeking God in all things*.
Lay people are writing authoritatively about Christian spirituality,
and they are looking to the tradition for an understanding of
Christian discipleship. I write out of that tradition, as part of it,
but above all as someone who realizes that it is leading me
inescapably into dialogue with the present day and with my lay
friends and colleagues. This conversation is proving fruitful in
every respect.

I have spoken to many other religious and lay people before
attempting to convey some of my own interpretations of the
tradition to paper. Many of them will recognize snatches of the

conversation here. The dialogue has been personally fruitful, if at times a little painful. All sharing means a little stripping. I have had to abandon some of the nice neat certainties and mysteries with which I shrouded my own life, while my lay friends have had to part with some of their sentimental ideas about nuns and priests. As many congregations form associations for lay people who wish to share their various spiritualities, and equally as lay people begin to reflect upon the value of their own place within the Christian tradition, perhaps the moment has come to bring some of these visions into the light.

For this reason I have chosen to write about a variety of contexts which belong to us all — namely the desert, mountain, valley, market place, universe and home — contexts in which God invites us all to live as chaste, poor and obedient people. These places have been hallowed in the tradition by the forms of religious life which emerged in each of them, but equally they exist in today's world and Church. They form our outer world but are mirrored in our inner world too. As such they are at once physical environments and internal images of who we are and how we may come to God. They provide the situations in which we do our Christian holding, owning and sharing.

I have been helped by many friends in the preparation of this book, notably my Provincial superior, Sister Francis North IBVM, by Ann Bromham IBVM, Mary Critchley, David Lonsdale SJ and Philip Sheldrake SJ with whom I work, by Judith Longman of SPCK and, incidentally, by Nilda Pettenuzzo DC, who invited me to talk to the Tite Street novices in the first place. Especial thanks must go to Gillian Orchard IBVM and Thomas Shufflebotham SJ who read the text for me in manuscript. Chapter nine originally appeared in a slightly different form in *The Way*, vol. 28 no. 4 (October 1988), under the title, 'And who lies broken at my gate?'.

1
Images of religious life

❧❦❧

My grandfather was one of seventeen children. One of the myths on which I was raised is that in later life these seventeen children, all of whom survived into adulthood, would telephone each other every Sunday afternoon to say what they had had for lunch, to share news and generally to pass the time of day. The experience of family life behind that practice is one of plenty. Plenty of children, plenty to eat and plenty of contact. There are other experiences of course. I remember watching an eighteen-year-old girl while she studied the maps in a careers prospectus. Her intention was to find the university which was furthest away from home and choose that. Her experience of family life had left her feeling stifled and with a strong and healthy desire to get away. We all have the experience — which may be good or bad — but we also carry images or understandings of family life which enable us to make sense of what is happening to us. These encode our private theology or way of understanding family life. They provide a personal frame of reference in terms of which we interpret our experience.

These images are not static like photographs. They are more like the moving pictures of a film, with close-ups and long-shots and treasured frames which we retain as stills. They affect our sense of place and inform our sense of what is appropriate and what might be inappropriate. Certain characters are highlighted at different moments, giving us insights into the importance of various roles and ways of behaving. We have individual images of what the words mother, father, sister and brother might mean. We envisage these people in relationship, with each other but also with us. We have certain understandings of where the family does its most intense living — at table for instance, or on holiday. Above all we have images of what it is to belong to our family, to form a good Christian family, and these, more than any of the others, are able to develop and change.

It is the beauty of personal theology, in common with all theology, that it is subject to change. It does not hold us or enable us to remain cocooned in past certainties. Theology is sustained by revelation and God's is a voice that both reveals the truth and calls us to deeper truth. We are always being asked to let go and to enter more deeply into the mystery of the otherness of God. Yet we do not experience this call in some sort of wasteland where God's is the only voice we hear. We experience it rather in the very fabric and pattern of our everyday lives which form the landscape for our journeying. That is why theology, which we have sometimes been tempted to limit to the formal teaching of our Churches, means listening to the questions we raise and the answers we give from the place where God is heard within.

Hence the importance of the teachings of the gospel and of our Churches. We are not asked to do our journeying alone, but always within the community of those who seek and those who find, being attentive to the voices of those who have sought and found and gone before us. Their dogmas must always inform our theologies, as must the reflections of those who are our fellow pilgrims, even if they are not necessarily our fellow believers.

Changing images

Much has been written recently about the moral and emotional development of young people, their cognitive development and their faith development and the place of the family within this process. Less has been written about corporate development, the life-cycle of the family as institution, and the patterns whereby any group or institution survives and renews itself down the generations. I belong to a religious congregation which is nearly four hundred years old. I can see evidence of times when we have survived and when we have retrenched, and times when we have renewed ourselves and been renewed. In my own family as well I can see evidence of the same kinds of patterns and I know from this experience that life comes most vigorously and is most fruitfully renewed at the times when the images change. For it is at these moments that our theology changes and is open to renewal in the light of a new call from God.

This is well illustrated by the apocryphal story of the young man who claimed, 'When I was seven I thought my parents knew everything. When I was seventeen I was convinced that they knew nothing. At twenty-seven I was round to borrow money off them and now that I'm thirty-seven I find myself calling them for advice on how to bring up my seventeen-year-old.' The relationship he was describing was underpinned by certain images. According to the first his parents were all-powerful and totally dependable and reliable. At seventeen, however, that image could not bear the weight of reality, so it was replaced by one which was equally unhelpful but equally strong. In time this image too was chased out by the facts and his parents became providers, initially of cash and ultimately of wisdom. In the case of these last two images, power was being correctly defined, transferred and appropriated. At the age of forty-seven I can only assume that the image would change again and would furnish a way to part with these parents by allowing them to grow old or to die.

The facts are kind. There are moments when it is helpful to stay with certain images because they continue to nurture us. There are times when it is more helpful to allow them to fragment and to move on to fresh understandings that will bring new life. Are there any signs that can help us to do this constructively? Does one start by looking at individual experience for guidelines or by looking at corporate experience? Or is the one to be validated only by testing it against the other? I remember the thrill I felt when I first saw that the development outlined by one school biology textbook enabled me to make sense of what I was learning in another. The one described the growth of the foetus from total dependence in saline solution within the mother's uterus through the budding of limbs to birth. Then came attempts to crawl and then to walk and so through childhood towards adult life. Elsewhere I was reading how this reality was lived out in the experience of the whole of the human race, in that our origins too were first in a formless sea where we struggled to learn to swim, to emerge on to the land, to crawl on four legs and then stand on two. Micro-development and macro-development provide models for each other.

I have since seen that this is what the two creation stories at the beginning of the book of Genesis are attempting to tell me. They are stories about our 'first parents' but they are also stories about ourselves. A good way of testing out what is happening in my life is to compare it with the wisdom I find there. Do I admit the existence within myself not only of light but also of chaos and dark and the place of God's spirit hovering over the waters of my un-formed self? Do I admit the existence in my own life of sin that is somehow original, belonging uniquely to me and which I try endlessly to project by claiming that the 'woman' or the 'serpent' did it, when in fact it lies deep within me and is an echo of my fear that I might not be like God?

A life lived in cycles

There are connections between the experience of individuals and that of groups. For this reason I have found it interesting to read what Joan Chittister, the American Benedictine, has to say in her analysis of the life cycles of religious institutions. In *Women, Ministry and Church* she sees their progress as follows. The first stage is the stage of origins, where the group is full of vitality and has a strong sense of purpose. Ordinarily there are a number of young people about, with all their idealism and energy. This leads inevitably to a period of expansion. New foundations proliferate, and new ideas are given shape and form in the most improbable of circumstances. This in turn gives way to a time of stabilization when choices will be made about where to live and how to live there, what to do and how to do it. Only in time — and that could mean anything up to several hundred years — will this system break down because the image no longer works. Then, inevitably, comes a time of transition. This will be marked by death, by a kind of minimal survival or by renewal.

One of the formative pictures which has made it possible for me to accept Chittister's analysis is that of the ruins of Cluny Abbey in France. Once the centre of twelfth-century monasticism, the hub of a universe which extended all over Europe, this monastery has become a landmark that pilgrims pass on their way to Taizé. Here the brothers have enlarged their church by adding on the canvas of a large circus tent. The ancient monastery with its beautiful stonework lies in ruins while young people stream in droves to pray in the less formal setting of Taizé. They sleep in tents on the hillside and eat from plastic trays. At Cluny, the vitality of the period of origin and expansion has gone; stabilization did not lead beyond itself and the energy to be inventive and to survive death was lost.

I find her analysis credible for a more important reason. The stages of origins, expansion, stabilization and breakdown can be used to describe the relationships most of us experience in our own families. They mirror the wider canvas of the experience of groups but they provide a framework within which to look at personal experience too. They remind us that tucked away inside these words are all the images we take for granted. Those that belong to the period of origins describe the nurturing role of parents, the dependency that is an integral part of early learning. There is a certain literalism there too, either because the parents have read all the right books about good-enough parenting and are anxious to get it right or because the facts dictate that this should be the case. A common experience is the experience of poverty. The novices to whom I first directed these thoughts recognized this as the outstanding connection between their own experience of origins in their families and the pattern they were aware of in their religious congregations. God the nurturer who inspires new forms of life does provide but seems also to be at pains to remind us that the quality of relationship is what counts rather than material benefits.

The next stage is the stage of expansion. When reflecting on their experience of family life the novices I was working with noted that this is a time of growth in understanding as well as in learning to walk and run. The freedom to enjoy greater physical mobility is accompanied by the freedom to think more broadly and more deeply. New models emerge as teachers and peers replace parents or share their role. New patterns of behaviour and access to the outer world become appropriate. Home opens up onto the world or at least onto the street outside. Similarly, the period of expansion which religious communities go through is marked by the same characteristics. The rules come to be written, relationships are defined — notably those which relate to the way in which authority is to be administered — and people work out their boundaries. They become clearer about what it is that makes the group distinctive, about what is 'us' and what is 'not us', what is 'me' and what is 'not me'. There is inevitably an element of tension in all of this. For what is 'me' can achieve a comforting and self-validating sense of superiority over what is 'not me'. Genuine boundaries — as opposed to inhibitions, blocks and barriers — are in any case incredibly difficult for us to erect, but they are essential for fully developed adult life. Families create them by ritualizing, by having certain things that the family members do together or always do at the same time or in the same way. These codes are essential because of the part they play in helping us define and defend our boundaries. Perhaps God too has boundaries and is anxious to prevent us from heaping either all the good or all the bad in the world onto a God we create ourselves. God the boundary-maker, like God the nurturer, offers us the wisdom of boundaries to contain the enthusiasm of expansion.

The religious group then moves on to a period of stabilization. This sounds touchingly like the middle years of most of us. It is not that we have less to bring to the service of the world and the Church, but rather that we have a more realistic idea about our capacities. It is not that we doubt the world's need of redemption, but more that we begin to know from our own experience that it is God who saves. We do not save ourselves. Ultimately the salvation of the world, even my treasured patch of it, is God's work, not my own. Stabilization can bring specialization, a keener and more insightful desire to enjoy intimacy with a few named friends rather than to love everyone — even 'for Jesus'. Stabilization can bring a sense of perspective, the wisdom that comes with years. But how is this sense of perspective to be renewed and to remain focused? How do groups avoid fossilizing into attitudes of complacency and self-righteousness? I heard of a woman who entered an enclosed monastery after practising as a dentist for a number of years. To her alarm she found that a community practice was to put sugar directly into the tea pot before the tea was poured. When she asked why this was done and suggested that nowadays sugar is regarded with a certain amount of caution and even alarm, she was told that 'we've always done it this way'. My hunch is that the practice probably dated from a time when sugar was rationed and that it proved a handy way of distributing the ration fairly, but in time the ritual had become fossilized and had acquired a life of its own. Yet we must assume that God the nurturer and boundary-maker is at work in this stage of the process as well, as the one who enables us to make patterns and rituals, the God of our security.

So why is it that our convents and monasteries are now full of rather elderly and rather tired people? What has happened to our security? I am lucky because, on occasion, I work with novices and see something of the idealism that inspires them. I could delude myself into thinking that there is no problem. My grandmother used to pray for vocations and regard me balefully when I told her that people were entering in droves in Asia, but that as far as Europe was concerned, her prayers remained unanswered. I could use these Indian and Korean vocations as an excuse for not facing the question of what is happening in Europe and North America. After all they bump up the statistics of any international congregation such as my own. And yet the facts are there and I cannot avoid them. I meet them in the sad eyes and weary shoulders of sisters who, during workshops and retreats, talk openly of their fears and misgivings about the future. Any animation is reserved for the stories they tell about the past, the good old days when God's sun shone in a bright and hopeful heaven. I meet them in the questions the administrators ask, about how to plan for survival and ensure the least suffering to the greatest number. I meet them when looking at local statistics and noting the changing age-structure they represent. There are congregations with one or two people aged under fifty and anything up to eighty or ninety aged over fifty. Where is our security? Where is God the nurturer and boundary-maker in all of this?

These facts must make us ask whether we are heading for death, minimal survival or renewal. The pattern of origins, expansion and stabilization matches our experience and now we are facing the Lent of the religious life. This is a place of stripping and transformation, a place where we are afraid to go. We forget that it is mirrored in the other patch of purple time the Churches give us, the time of the waiting womb which we call Advent. Where Lent and Advent are allowed to speak to each other like this the image of transformation can take some hold of our imaginations. For if the messages of Lent are about a suffering God who mourns and grieves with us, the messages of Advent are about a God who prepares for new birth. This is a God who builds a nest and prepares a layette and dreams about the lovely child that will be born.

God the image-maker

Our mistake is to be endlessly cheerful and pretend that there is nothing the matter. Our mistake is not to allow ourselves to grieve and mourn the passing of our certainties and so come before God the image-maker with open hands. Our personal experience is that we hold the treasure of our lives in earthenware vessels. Why did we expect the treasure of the religious life to be different? Our personal experience is of sin, of fragmentation and failure, of separation. In our own lives we know that we must not be afraid of these or disown them because otherwise we cannot pray, 'I know that my redeemer lives' (Job 19.25) and know that he is alive and is at work in our lives. Above all we know that it is all right to grow up and move away from home and family. Of course there will be instances where this leads to death; of course there will be cases of minimal survival. These are familiar to us from our experience of the human story and may have been lived out in our own story too. But the natural term towards which the growth process moves, the natural development of the lovely child is towards life and change. The facts of the matter are that moving away from home energizes people and sets them free. From our experience of natural development we can recall how important this separation is and what a birth it represents.

God the image-maker can offer us a new vision. It could be that this will take us to places we never thought to visit, to experiences we never thought to have, to a series of images which will necessarily change the way religious communities live and move and have their being. Who is the God who asks this of us? What is God's will? I believe that we are being called at the moment — and maybe as never before — by God the image-maker.

At each of the stages I have outlined our sets of images had internal coherence. At the time of origins our first founders knew that they had to experiment. The images of poverty, chastity and obedience with which they worked, or their understanding of the place of some form of distinctive house and life-style, or even dress, were at once given to them and offered to them for transformation and innovation. As they expanded and became more established and took on the responsibility for forming the next generation they had to codify these images and spell out their inner coherence. At the time of stabilization they were thought to be definitive. Now we are being shown that this is not the case. In 1974 I walked through Selfridges, the big department store in London, wearing a long black habit and veil and heard a woman say in proprietary tones, 'How nice, a real nun'. She would not recognize me now; I barely recognize myself. The images have changed and are changing still. So what are the lessons of history? What can my understanding of the religious life of the past feed into my present-day understanding? How can the wisdom of the past inform the future? Where has God the image-maker been at work before? How can I recognize the Advent signs through the pain of Lent?

If there is a vision for sharing within the community of believers, whether religious or lay, what is it and where does it lie?

2

Into the desert

❦

The desert is both a place and an attitude. The religious life began
in the desert, in a setting where people could make connections
between the desert outside and the desert within, the desert of
solitude and the desert of desire. Christianity began in the desert
too; the gospels begin with John the Baptist's call to repentance
from the heart of the Judean wilderness. The learning we do in
external deserts enables us to visit the desert we carry within, in
spite of our natural dread and anxiety, for in these deserts we
learn to contemplate and to discern. We learn to look at the world
through the eyes of God and to see the hand of God in all that
happens there. For this reason the desert tradition cries out for
interpretation and understanding as it has so much to say to our
contemporary search for God. The men and women who first
chose to seek God in the desert have a message today for lay
people and religious alike.

The secrets of the sands

Finding deserts today appears not to be such an easy business. Yet
they do exist and our experience is full of them. When we learn to
recognize them we can learn their mysteries, the wisdom of the
sands. They range from obvious ones, the literal deserts of the
tradition, to the deserts we have created in making barren urban
landscapes and isolating ourselves from our senses. Deserts may
be remote, lonely places or familiar places close to home —
anywhere I choose to be alone. I have a friend who has a photo in
her room of a stretch of arid Californian desert where she spent
time alone. I have comparable pictures, photographs of scenes
where I have spent moments which have stilled me and enabled
me to notice, observe and reflect. On my desk I have a picture of
the Hampshire downs, a view of a wheatfield which is golden and

green and fades into a blue sky. I have it there because it is full of memories for me. It evokes the afternoon I spent in that field and the thoughts and feelings which were passing through my mind that day. It reminds me of my capacity to slow down and to contemplate the gift of God in natural beauty. But I have other desert images in my memory as well.

One is of driving through Belfast and of being unable to get to where I wanted to be. At the end of every northbound street I met a concrete wall built to isolate one part of the population from the other. There were children playing in this desert, little ragamuffins who ran out fearlessly, virtually under the wheels of my car. I felt fear because the walls of the houses were covered in graffiti that spoke of an anger and pain I found quite shocking. I felt fear because I had been in Londonderry that morning and had gazed into the barrel of a gun held by a lad of nineteen in an armoured car and mounted there for my protection. I felt fear because my voice sounds English and belies my roots in Irish Roman Catholicism. Yet I felt anger too and indignation at my own ignorance. I had to touch the wounds of Christ before I could believe and when I did touch them in the experience of the people I observed in Northern Ireland I was slow to recognize the Lord. That desert too had lessons I needed to learn.

Earlier there had been a less localized desert, one whose extent was in time rather than space. I had lived in the desert of three years of regular travel on the London Underground, shoulder to shoulder with complete strangers, finding myself locked in the embrace of their newspapers and briefcases. The few who spoke to me I remember quite clearly, even at fifteen years remove: the woman who was smoking dried lettuce leaves, the man who was selling dirty postcards and pocketed them before coming over to give me a ten-pence piece because I was wearing a habit and he was no doubt a good Catholic. I remember too the desolation of missing trains or of falling asleep from exhaustion and waking with a jolt.

There have been other deserts as well, the obvious ones of retreats and days of recollection fed by images of withdrawal and calm. These were often illusory oases of chronic boredom and did not hold the rewards all the introverts had promised me would be there. We often romanticize the desert by assuming that the act of withdrawal will magically pull God out of the air, failing to find the God who is the air we breathe and the gift of life on every breath. By emphasizing the experience of *withdrawal from* rather than that of *engaging with*, we have failed to learn one of the most important lessons of the desert tradition. Equally, however, there has been the desert of death, of seeing an empty bed where once I sat and chatted and laughed with a friend. There has been the desert of separation, of saying goodbye in airports and sobbing quietly in the departure lounge. There has been the desert of denial and the desert of betrayal, my own as well as other people's.

In each of these I have been forced to gaze on reality and see it with clear eyes. I have been forced to go beyond the obvious categories whereby we imagine that to be alone we have to avoid the crowd; or that to be in the desert we have to leave the city; or that to be people who meet God we have to avert our eyes from everyone else. Our experience dictates otherwise. We know the place of solitude and how it differs from loneliness; we know the place of simplicity and how it differs from penury; we know the place of anxiety and dread, of ecstasy and longing and how these differ from the more mundane reactions we ordinarily allow ourselves to have. Loneliness, penury and the mundane may be ways in to these deeper experiences, yet once we have visited them we know the difference and cannot easily go back. We are 'ill at ease in the old dispensation' because we have met the Lord of the new. For this reason real deserts are needed and we must go into them to learn what it is they have to teach us. They exist within us and in our outer experience and both must be visited. But this is only so that we can use the wisdom we gain in the desert to move back into the world of our everyday living and continue to apply its messages there. Real deserts are where we learn to contemplate and to discern; to know the difference and to tell the difference. If we return to the world of our everyday living as contemplative discerning people, as people who know and can tell, then we have learnt the secrets of the sands.

In the beginning

The desert tradition is a venerable one. It forms part of the Christian tradition and remains part of it. Why did people go off into the desert? Why do they continue to do so? Various theories have been advanced to explain why Christians in the fourth century took to the desert in such large numbers and why the origins of the religious life are ordinarily dated from this time. The most convincing explanations seem to be speaking of something we can still recognize today. The emperor Diocletian died in the year 310. After his death Christians were no longer persecuted and were able to take their place as honourable members of society. The words 'martyr' and 'Christian' had been inextricably linked in the self-understanding of the early Church. Yet it was not some horrible masochism that led the first solitaries to take to the wilderness in search of austerity. Nor did they withdraw into the wilderness because the danger had gone out of Christian living or because city life failed to fire their understanding of radicality.

They went because they wished to engage with the forces of evil, not because they sought to flee from them. The gospels had demonstrated that the desert is the place where evil spirits dwell (Mark 1.13) and they went out in quest of them with the imagination and enthusiasm of any crusader. In this they were imitating Jesus who began his public ministry by also going out into the place of temptation and hearing the call of sin. But theirs was not a fundamentalist interpretation of what he did. Nor was it a romantic re-reading of his prayer that his disciples might be preserved from the world. It is we who so readily set up dichotomies and imagine that they were fleeing from the city into some sunlit wilderness where they could re-create the Garden of Eden away from the corruption of city life. I believe theirs to have been a much saner view, one which did not set up an opposition between the natural things which God makes and those which are the 'work of human hands'.

What matters is the quest, not the place where the questing is done. The quest committed them to search for the good in a place where they could be certain of meeting evil. Only in this way could they be sure of learning the exact nature and place of each and of learning to tell the difference between the two. Only in this way could they be sure that this learning would be internalized, that they would come to know their own goodness and their own sinfulness. Neither could be projected out onto an unwitting world; both had to be acknowledged and owned, held and contained. For this reason many of the early anchorites exhibited really strange behaviour. The greatest oddball of them all was subsequently canonized by the Church and that should give us pause. In these post-Freudian days we would use some interesting words to describe the personality of a Simon Stylites. Yet on the top of his pillar and in his obsession for building ever taller pillars he was exploring depths within himself most of us would not care to acknowledge, let alone to proclaim to the world in such grandly phallic fashion.

The place of spiritual direction

As Church and State made peace the anchorite movement spread. Its eventual presence in England is commemorated by the pubs called 'The Anchor' that litter our landscape. Many of these are far away from the sea or navigable rivers and serve to remind us of the solitaries who kept the desert tradition alive in our midst. The irony of pubs taking the name from anchorites is not meant to set up some false antithesis. I am reminded of the story of two Jesuit novices. One asked his novice master if he might smoke while he prayed and received the answer 'No'; his young companion on the other hand asked if he might pray while he smoked and received the answer 'Yes'.

The solitaries who sought God in the wilderness prayed while they worked. Manual labour entitled them to survive but also gave them a context within which to discern God's will. For manual labour involves choices, not dramatic ones admittedly, but daily ones with demonstrable consequences. Another context was that afforded by spiritual direction, for a mitigated form of the anchorite life soon developed. Anchorites grouped together in order to attach themselves to someone who would guide them in their Christian living and so they became cenobites. The many voices they heard in the heart of their solitude cried out for interpretation with the result that they looked for individuals who would teach them how to discern the voice of God in what they found there.

Pachomius, who is sometimes called the father of the religious life, had charge of some five thousand monks from Tabennisi in Egypt by the year 315. He wrote a rule for them organizing their life in detail and introduced the idea of a minister or administrator who would have charge of the day-to-day running of their property. In effect this guaranteed that he would be free to attend to the work he had undertaken to do on their behalf as their spiritual father or *hegoumene*. This solution seems enviable from our vantage point. I have several friends, men and women committed to the justice issues raised by Christian feminism, who have confessed to me that what they really need is a wife. Pachomius knew how difficult it is to do the shopping and cleaning and cook the meals and catch up on the ironing, and so he chose a solution which divided this labour off from his 'ministry'. It is a solution that looks attractive but which creates as many problems as it solves. For what messages are being given when the physical is divided from the spiritual like this? How is it possible to avoid demeaning the one when the other is given priority? How can a spiritual director claim that discernment is about hearing the voice of God in one's everyday experiences if his own are so very rarefied? I think this division of labour lies behind the rigid distinction which subsequently developed between what is prayer and what is not. We would need a Julian of Norwich to remind us that 'in the same instant and place in which our soul is made sensual, in that same instant and place exists the city of God, ordained for him from without beginning' (*Showings*, long text, chapter 55). This is the remark of someone who has met God while doing the ironing or the washing up, as well as while thinking about sex or food.

I have said that Pachomius had undertaken to do this work on their behalf. This careful phrasing conceals a question which has equal relevance nowadays as spiritual direction becomes more and more accessible to religious and lay people alike. How do people know if they are being called to be spiritual directors? How do they start? The marks of an authentic call seem to be that the person in question is chosen. There is a sense in which they find that they are doing spiritual direction before they even know that such a thing exists. They are the natural listeners, the people we turn to in distress or with our problems. The desert tradition has something useful to say in so far as it spells out certain guidelines. Spiritual direction is both an art and a science. The natural listeners have an advantage. They are gifted in one of the basic skills that make it an art. Yet they have to know what they are listening for and so they need the science that must accompany their gift. The desert tradition is clear about the contents of this science and its insights remain valid nowadays. The early anchorites were advised to look for three things in the people they went to for spiritual direction: a knowledge of theology, of

cardiognosis and of *diacrisis*. In plain English, this means that
they should know something about God, something about people
and something about how we communicate with God and how
God communicates with us.

Only the director who gave evidence of these characteristics
would attract groups of cenobites and would in turn be able to
impose certain criteria on them. The anchorite was supposed to
exercise a completely free choice of director and to look only for
the best. There is no point in choosing an easy option. People
look for spiritual direction for a variety of reasons. There are
those who seek guidance in prayer, those who are facing changes
and choices, and those who come because they have been sent —
perhaps as part of their religious formation or theological training.
There are others who seek direction because it looks 'safe' whereas
in fact they need psychotherapy or pastoral counselling. In each
case the requirement is the same; each of these people should be
free to choose the director and have as clear an idea as possible of
what they need without trivializing it. There is the further
understanding that they should then abide by their choice
faithfully, even when the going gets tough because the director's
imperfections — or their own — are revealed. There is nothing
worse than the individual who goes priest- or nun-hopping. I say
this not because I believe that priests or nuns necessarily make
good directors, but because they are the most usual target for this
particular activity. The final insight from the tradition is that the
relationship should be one of love, not fear, and based on complete
openness. Such openness enables whatever work there is to be
done to surface more quickly than might otherwise be the case. It
has to be matched by an equal commitment to confidentiality.

In this way it becomes possible to journey through three stages
both in this relationship and in the relationship it mirrors, which
the one being directed enjoys with God. This insight has a
contemporary ring. It acknowledges the mechanisms which
nowadays we call projection and transference and understands
that the director will have iconic status at times and must be
aware of it. By this I mean that the director will become someone
through whom the love of God is made especially accessible to
whoever is being directed. Equally spiritual direction is seen
within the context of growth; thus we have a model of personal

faith development which can usefully dialogue with some of our twentieth-century ones.

The first stage in the relationship envisaged by the desert tradition is that of master and slave. These are not words with which we are particularly comfortable nowadays. They serve to remind us that the written records were prepared by men for whom the comparison with slavery was a natural one. The same relationship of teacher to learner no doubt existed in the women's tradition but the vocabulary they used to describe it has been lost to us. At this stage there is learning to be done. The knowledge of God, of self and of the way God communicates with us have to be uncovered. I say uncovered because the director's task at this stage is to help those being directed to see what images or understandings of God operate in their lives. What is their self-image like? How do they pray? In this way the theology, *cardiognosis* and *diacrisis* of the director are being shared with the one who is directed. If the master is one who shares with his slave the image can remain, but if he exploits the good will of a generous individual, then it must go.

In the second stage of the relationship the desert tradition talks about a master/faithful servant relationship. This has gospel antecedents: the faithful servant is a freeman who in effect controls his master's household. The image is alien to our culture but I would still like to preserve the insight it conceals because once again I see it as a description of how power is to be shared. Nothing is worse than the spiritual director who sets up as a guru and fails to see the ministry of spiritual direction in terms of service. It is also hopelessly dishonest not to admit that the relationship is one where people could play particularly sinister power games. For this reason supervision is essential, so that the director is accountable and can be challenged. The supervision I have in mind is that which anyone in the wider world of pastoral care takes for granted, that is to say supervision of oneself and one's work.

The final stage is that of parent and child. The image is one of both nurture and freedom. It is not intended to depict any kind of dependency; instead the movement envisaged by this model of development is movement into what the tradition has sometimes called 'indifference'. This means something far removed from the cold lack of involvement the word normally conveys: it is about caring passionately and at the same time being free from one's passion, about a mobility and independence of judgement which make relationships utterly honest and truthful. The daughter or son of the house has a totally different relationship to her or his parents from that of a slave. As children of the family they share its story because they are its story. This is their inheritance. They are the contemplatives and the people who can choose freely because they have learnt to discern.

A *living tradition*

I have suggested that the desert remains central to the Christian tradition because we still experience the lure of solitude, of being alone with God. In our experience the desert stands in contrast to the rest of our world. It is like the times we give to personal prayer compared with the rest of our lives. We hunger for the simplicity it represents and the closeness it seems to guarantee to all that we most treasure. We know that in our own deserts we still hear the call of God. Hosea's words, 'Therefore, behold, I will allure her, and bring her into the wilderness, and speak tenderly to her' (Hosea 2.14), set up resonances deep within us.

The early desert mothers and fathers have a further lesson for us however. Where we seek to share their vision, its place in the Christian tradition proves to be even more central than we imagine. They lived in the desert, they did not just visit. They could not divide up their experience, saying God is in this part of it and not in that. God is in the desert bits, the times when I pray alone, the times when I withdraw and live more simply, the times when I experience my own solitude; but God is in the rest as well. The desert tradition in the history of the religious life has something incredibly important to say to the way we live nowadays. The early mothers and fathers de-mythologized the desert, but because we only visit it and do not live there we are tempted to give it almost magical powers. In this way we miss the point. The lessons of the sands are about learning there how to search for God in our most intimate reactions, so that we can contemplate the God who is all the time labouring in our midst. The wisdom of the sands is about letting this God inform our choices so that we live our lives in harmony with God's will. The secrets of the sands are about containing our projections, and learning the place of strength and the place of weakness, of good and of evil. The desert is both a place and an attitude, but above all it is a task.

3

Onto the mountain

❦

Every Christian community is invited to be a 'school of the Lord's service', where each member may 'run with unspeakable sweetness of love in the way of the Lord's commandments'. These words from the Prologue to St Benedict's Rule describe a total environment, the kind of place in which the task of coming before God as one is rather than as one might like to be is made easier because we do not come alone. Our model for human relationships is one of intimacy, the model put before us by the God who is Trinity. In our search for this God we are all the time drawn into relationships and invited to find God within them rather than apart from them. The mountain tradition in Christian spirituality is as old as the tradition itself because Jesus too went up mountains in order both to find God (Mark 9.2-8) and to communicate the heart of his message (Matthew 5—7); Jesus too chose disciples (Matthew 4.18-22), looked to intimate relationships with the women and men who were his friends and was helped and sustained by them (John 19.25-27).

The mountain is at once an image of apartness and of vision. The apartness is typified in the history of the religious life by those who down the centuries have gone apart from the world of everyday living to create community. They have set up specialized environments in which all the dramas of the human family are lived out in microcosm, rather than in the context of the wider world. At the same time, however, they have been saying something important about the place of a new vision of human living to which they aspire. This vision belongs in a very special way to the mountain tradition. Each of us needs to go up mountains to gain a different perspective on reality from the one we have down on the plain. As a child I lived at the foot of the Mendips and can recall the thrill I felt when I was told that they were the foothills of the Alps. From one hill in particular there was a view which stretched right across to Exmoor, a two-hour drive away. The little orchards of Somerset which ordinarily contained my world-view shrank to nothing in comparison; Glastonbury Tor which appeared enormous from my bedroom window marked barely a ripple on the landscape. A life lived on the mountain top can of course turn in on itself and create its own diminished world-view. At its best, however, it offers the world the promise that human community is both desirable and possible. It has a message for the rest of us.

So much for the external image. The mountain tradition also affords us an internal one. We talk about peak-experiences, moments of heightened awareness and personal transfiguration when we know we are on holy ground, that gives us greater access to God. What does the movement of religious men and women into community have to say to these?

Benedict (*c*.480–547) gave the mountain tradition a certain shape and form and his Rule (535–540) is the most complete statement of its dynamics which is available to us. What insights does this Rule offer us in our seeking and making community wherever we are gathered and in the deep search of the human heart for an intimacy which will bring us to God and God to us?

The search for community

In common with each of us Benedict was formed by early influences. He was raised and educated in Rome, an imperial city still ruled by senate and consuls. A communitarian model was normative for him and yet he ran away from this. He spent three years in solitude at Subiaco before being persuaded to become abbot there and subsequently at the monastery he founded at Monte Cassino. His own progress was in effect the exact opposite of what he described in his Rule: 'After long probation in a monastery . . . go out from the ranks of the community to the solitary combat of the desert' (ch. 1, 1). I like to think of Benedict distilling his understanding of community during his three years of solitude and later extracting the wisdom which would ensure that while Rome decayed, his own people would have something more enduring to live by. I also observe here the wisdom which would legislate not from a general norm, but in terms of individuals.

Benedict made certain innovations in the practice of those cenobites who continued to carry on the desert tradition. He envisaged a monarchical abbot who would be elected for life and who in turn would appoint his own officials. Such institutionalizing of power has to be girded about with checks and balances and in the case of the abbot this is done by giving him a very precise brief. His function within the community is defined in the second chapter of the Rule: 'Let him always remember that he has undertaken the government of souls and will have to give an account of them.' The abbot does not stand at the end of a long chain of command, God does — and the abbot is accountable to God. The other principal mechanism which ensures that it is safe to put so much power in the hands of one man is that Benedict legislates for two levels of council or consultation. All the brethren are to be consulted on major matters of common interest and there are to be smaller meetings of senior monks for less important matters. I find this intriguing as it goes against our contemporary understanding of corporate management. We are inclined to keep big decisions for the people at the top and to fob off juniors — younger children in the family, junior executives — by consulting them only on small issues. Worst of all, we are inclined not to distinguish between big and little decisions and to fall into the fatal trap of treating every decision as though it were a major one. In this way we give too much time to small decisions and avoid major ones, allowing them to rumble on like an inflamed appendix while the years go by.

I have seen more blood shed in convents over the allocation of cupboard space and clothes than I have seen spent addressing the major questions that relate to witness and work, life and life-style. I have seen remarkable consultation as well, and been tantalized when the opportunities it affords are ignored by those being consulted. Of course it is easier to get other people to make decisions for you, then you can grouse at them — or as Benedict put it 'murmur' — for the rest of your days. Of course it is easier to set people up and turn them into the enemy than to face the enemy within. I find Benedict's insight extraordinarily powerful, precisely because it legislates for a responsible use of power. Small decisions can safely be delegated and those who make them be encouraged to develop skills appropriate to the task: the man who is sub-cellarer is allowed to develop a nose; the one who is guest master is encouraged to become an expert on duvet tog marks. Why burden the entire community with the responsibility of carrying this much information around when one or two people can do it so more effectively? Energy is correctly focused where major questions are addressed and there the wisdom of the whole group is needed, and must be used.

When I was a young nun I used to think that the will of God lived on my novice mistress's desk in a little box. She alone had access to it. If I wanted to know it I had to ask her what it was and how I might do it. In this way I was denying my own place within the decision-making process and setting her up to fail. In fact she was a kind and moderate woman, so nothing went very wrong. The God whom I feared to be at work as I misread religious obedience like this was a God of secrets rather than a God of mystery, a God whose place in my own story I was strenuously denying. Later I thought the will of God was more like the smile of the Cheshire Cat in *Alice in Wonderland*, that it was somehow 'out there' and that I and my legitimate religious superiors had to search for something which might, in the event, prove unknowable because it would vanish every time any of us approached it. Once again this misreading had certain attractions. I could still blame other people for getting it wrong. Above all I could blame God and continue to ignore what I was hearing from within of what God's will might be for me.

Nowadays I believe that the will of God lies within and that I can know it only when I attempt to discern it in dialogue with other people. I am returning to Benedict's insight about the place of community. By within I mean within me and within the world, within the Church and within my religious congregation. We all need to listen to each other in order for this voice of God to have shape and form, pitch and resonance, and for it to be addressed to the real questions our Churches and world are asking. Moreover these big questions can be disentangled from the little ones. As I reflect on this image of the will of God I am reminded of nothing so much as the Japanese Zen garden. In it there are seventeen stones arranged in such a way that no single visitor to the garden, no gardener or resident tramp can see all of them at once. The perspective of each is limited. When they begin to talk to each other and notably when they risk staying where they are in the garden rather than moving into the security of some nice

27

conference hall, then the shape and form of the garden, the place and pattern of its every stone are revealed.

So too, I believe, with the will of God, which was first made known to us in quite another garden and still seeks to be known and lived in our midst. When religious communities undertake together to listen to this voice and hear what it is saying about faith and justice, about being non-possessive and non-manipulative and not abusing power, then they are in a position to have some very interesting and radical things to say and Benedict's insight is given an appropriate context. And the same is true of all Christian communities. They are places where the will of God can be known because two or three are gathered there in the Lord's name, and his promise is, 'There am I in the midst of you' (Matthew 18.20), there am I within you.

This finding of God and God's will within is given a context by Benedict's other main innovatory practice. The monks' formal hours of prayer are laid out in some detail in his Rule and this formal prayer time is contextualized by the rhythms of the rest of their day. The *Opus Dei* or work of God that they do consists both of time spent praying the psalms and listening to God's word in the Scriptures and of time spent working with their hands. It takes years for the psalms to sink in, for their vocabulary and imagery to become part of one's mental furniture, and part of the air one breathes. It takes years for the truths about God which they present to become part of how we relate to the world. The psalms integrate; they admit every human feeling and emotion; they enable me to come before God as I am, rather than as I imagine I ought to be; they use images from sea and land, earth and sky with equal ease; they recall a God who is involved in the human story because this God made the human condition and loves us all. This is a God who has arms, hands and fingers, a God who touches and is in touch with the fabric of our lives. Where this God is gradually recognized and known by a whole group of people who share a common form of prayer, then this prayer with its familiar images begins to affect their entire way of being in the world.

Manual labour, work done with real arms and hands and fingers likewise affects the way we relate to the world. Recently I was giving a retreat to a group of young women from the Student Christian Movement during which we worked with lovely cool, clean clay. There was very little conversation, just a concentration of force and energy and a coming to insight based on the wisdom that lies captured inside one half of our heads and is so rarely allowed to inform what we think and do. The left hemisphere controls our verbal activity and so most of our thinking. The right hemisphere, on the other hand, looks after our pictures and symbols, our dreams and aspirations. I am always shocked to find how right-handed I am. I know that the theory is that the left hemisphere is tied to the right-hand side of the body, but to have this confirmed so clearly by my own hands is really frightening. My poor weak left hand demonstrates to me all too clearly that I live out of one side of my head only. This is an imbalance I have yet fully to understand. All I know for the moment is that Benedict has something to tell me here too, for his intention was to say something about the value of manual labour by having people work with their hands.

The place of community

People who do not live in monasteries and convents sometimes have rather an idealized image about what this must be like. Yet their own experience should give them pause. Equally, monks and nuns can have a very idealized picture of family life. And yet their experience too should give them pause. It is incredibly difficult to form Christian community because we are so bad about giving space to the dark as well as to the light, to anger and fear as well as to peace and joy. The Churches have thrived for far too long on the myth of denial and have enabled their members to repress what they either know or fear to be true about themselves and caused this to be swathed in secrecy. Community is essential to the mountain image of religious life, whether this be the hallowed mountain of Monte Cassino where Benedict began or the more modern mountains where his present-day followers make their homes; and all of us have an experience of community because we all began life in some kind of family. Families are not ordinarily idealized by their members; most of us have a fairly sane and balanced view of our families as contexts where we belong, warts and all. At home I can take my shoes off and slouch around in old clothes. In theory at least, I can *be* without having to *do*. But it is more complicated than this. I must be on my guard as well, because here I am known as in no other context. This could be delightful and liberating, but it is potentially toxic as well. At home I know that we are supported by a common myth. My sister and two brothers and I were raised on the same stories and we care about the same kinds of things, we have the same mannerisms and many of the same illusions. Blood is thicker than water. Yet equally we know where to put the boot in and our methods of attack and defence are likely to be fairly savage because one way and another we really know too much about each other. My sister used to be able to reduce me to paroxysms of embarrassment and rage by commenting that it was such a shame that I'd wet my nappy at my christening. She is my godmother and so she knew. Denial and repression become difficult if not impossible in the face of this kind of knowledge because it antedates the knowledge I claim to have about myself.

I, for one, have been slow to allow this experience of family and the realities of family life to inform my understanding of Christian community in the sense of religious congregation or Church. I still idealize far too easily and catch myself denying the right of 'religious people', myself included, to be weak and imperfect, to make mistakes and own a 'shadow'. Popular myths about religious are very strong, any 'church person' is under some kind of compulsion to be good and holy. So we have enormous difficulty approaching God as we really are and creating a climate in which we can respect each other's needs for both intimacy and privacy.

Our need for intimacy is to do with belonging and lies at the heart of the mountain tradition. Our need for privacy is there as well, however, and requires some kind of clarification. Any understanding of family life or community life which sets up the collective at the expense of the personal will meet with problems. Benedict legislated for differences in age, gifts and spiritual capacity. He provided for different needs by allowing each of his monks sufficient sleep, food and clothing. Where men undertook by a vow of stability to live together, certain safeguards had to be built into the system which would enable them to survive as individuals and also be able to participate in whatever they did in common. The impression of community which we have when we see monks gathering to say their office together, whether on television or in the flesh, is one of anonymity. And this is appropriate at that moment of their day; the religious habit, after all, began life as a nice warm overcoat to wear in choir. The sense of community which they convey at other times is decidedly more eclectic. One of my earliest memories is of the braces with which a monk who came to stay at our house kept up his pyjama bottoms. This too has its place and it would be a great shame if God were depicted as preferring only the strictly unzany.

If Benedict legislated for differences, he also provided a context in which the truth could be aired and dysfunction given a name. The Chapter of Faults gives people a chance to say this out loud in public to the brethren. It enables them to itemize their mistakes, to own their weakness and if necessary their despair, and it remains a very simple but very wise piece of legislation. Darkness and light may be held in harmony where both are admitted. What is dangerous is to try to live exclusively in the light.

Community and the place of prayer

While the monastic life is well-adjusted to balancing the individual and the group by prizing both equally, monastic prayer has certain other qualities which make it an attractive option to other non-monastic groups. At its most developed it has passed to us through the unlikely hand of Cranmer in the two services which form the backbone of the Church of England Book of Common Prayer, namely Mattins and Evensong. The liturgy of the monastic hours is there set out for Anglican clergy as the normative way of praying. This is an attractive proposition for people who live an ordered life, whose work patterns are regular and whose days and nights are marked off quite literally by the patterns of light and darkness. For this reason too the monastic qualities of peace and stability are likely to be prized in homes where there is the same sense of order and pattern and purpose. These are contexts in which prayer and life are marked by the same qualities, places where there is harmony between the two.

Because the community or family model of praying and living is so compelling, it is tempting to allow it to become so mainstream as to preclude any other human groupings. Other forms of the religious life will be looked at in this book: ones which speak to the experiences of childless couples, single people and people who choose to live in other groups. For the moment, however, my intention is to point out some of the ways in which it is inappropriate to try to make the Benedictine experience more than Benedict himself intended that it should be. A 'school of the

Lord's service' is a developmental environment, one in which people are encouraged to come to self-knowledge and to relationship. The mountain may be a place for meeting God — as indeed it was for Moses (Exodus 3) and Elijah (1 Kings 19), amongst others — but it is also a place for meeting other people. The community or family model is essentially a circular model. How do we treat people who do not belong to our circle? How do we treat those who, while still wishing to form such a circle with us, are looking outwards from the group, or beyond the group? How do we treat those who wish to belong for a while and then move on?

The Christian Churches have a problem with these people, so it is inevitable that religious communities should as well, as do families. The experience of belonging for a while in a deliberate manifestation of Christian community and then moving on is an increasingly familiar one because patterns which are appropriate to times of formation are later found to be unsuitable. Benedict made provision for this: monasticism was seen as provisional, as preparation for the solitary life. His understanding can inform our own, including some of our contemporary and more complex notions of whatever a solitary life might mean. Our problem, if we have one, is that we try to make everything normative, whereas the essence of Christian living is that it is always provisional. We are people who are asked to pray 'Thy Kingdom come' in both the 'already here' and the 'not yet' mode. Benedictine monasticism has much to say to our dilemma. From the mountain top it is possible to offer wisdom to the world, but eventually the world too has its wisdom and this nudges its way forward for our attention.

4

The valley and beyond

❦

When the world nudges in, what begins to happen? By the twelfth
century it was becoming clear that religious, economic, social and
cultural factors all have their part to play in the way we come
before God. We are the 'material people in a material world' of
the popular song, even when we attempt to turn our backs on this
material world.

Material people in a material world

No religious order demonstrates this totally, but each of the great
orders of the tenth to twelfth centuries highlights aspects of the
way in which we are people of our age. I find this reassuring; it
reminds me of something I learnt only when I arrived at university
in the late sixties. There I discovered that a phenomenon which I
had imagined was true only of my friends in the religious life had
some kind of universal application. I do not know where my head
had been: in some kind of sand I suppose. But in a college context
I discovered the same idealism, impulsive generosity, quest for
the beyond, and desire to experiment and to learn by doing that
had led my contemporaries in the convent and myself into our
particular version of the journey. The most impressive student in
my year was a young man who was reading Geography. He
belonged to the Salvation Army, had friends who would play
mournful hymns with him on silver trombones during the lunch
break and seemed to be in endless conflict with authority. From
one end he was castigated for attending the college eucharist and
from the other he was regarded as a rabble rouser for the
enthusiasm with which he got us to campaign for good and
inevitably political causes.

I recognized in him some of the idealism I knew from within

myself. I recognized it in other people too: men and women who would have claimed no formal kind of church membership. I spent the month of June 1968 in Paris, stepping my way over piles of damaged paving stones in the Latin Quarter, avoiding the debris as glasscutters replaced smashed and boarded-up windows and noticing the graffiti which warned me to be careful, because 'Ears have walls'. The following term we all became political animals and by the end of the year were singing the 'Internationale' while walking down the road from a party our professor had held to wish us well. It all sounds very 'sixties' now, and so it was. The seventies had a smart word to describe the phenomenon, 'conscientization', a mushrooming of similar ideas at a certain moment in history, in different places all over the world, a sharing of hope and vision that overcomes the more obvious divides imposed by Church or nation. For a brief moment it seems as though there may indeed be a 'music of the spheres', that we all hear at once.

The medieval world demonstrated both the fanciful and the factual sides of this possibility. Gossuin de Mès, a historian, wrote an encyclopaedia in verse form called *Discours sur le monde*. In it he described this music by saying that no one who hears it would ever want to go against God's will. Children hear it in their sleep, he claimed, and this is why they laugh at night. Fanciful perhaps, but nevertheless a striking image. The more factual side of inter-connectedness is easier to verify. The monks of Cluny learnt about 'federation' from their world, and so it is not surprising that the monastic 'daughter-houses' founded or reformed from this monastery rose from 60 in 1049 to 2000 in 1109. The feudal values of contemporary society informed their practice too and gave them a machine of extraordinary power and influence in Europe.

Equally, it is not surprising that when Bruno (1035–1101) and his six companions struck out against such power by going off to the Chartreuse valley to combine elements of both the eremetical and cenobitic forms of the religious life, they too developed a model which in fact drew heavily on contemporary culture. Each monk would live alone; studying, praying, working, sleeping and eating in his little three-roomed cell. This had an oratory or prayer-room, a workshop and a bedroom and a little garden and made the monk something of a peasant smallholder. However he also had his place in the abbey church where he would meet his brethren for Mass and recite the office. On Sundays and feast days he would also eat with them. A very tough life, but a mixed one, except that even the mixing was hardly convivial. The climate was one of prayer, solitude and simplicity, a reclaiming of essentials in a world where the lives of the many and the few were in stark contrast.

The valley as image

We owe the word Cistercian to another valley, the valley at Cîteaux where Robert de Molesme (1028–1112) set up his community in 1098 with twenty companions. In this valley the image comes into its own. I have ambiguous feelings about whatever it is that the valley represents, inspired largely by a French First World War poem. It has echoes of Siegfried Sassoon's 'Why do you lie with your legs ungainly huddled?' but starts on a quite different note, evoking the colours of a summertime green valley with a silver stream running through it. Yet the golden-haired young man who lies asleep beside the water has two red holes in his head. The valley is one of promise and it contains this shock. Valleys can shelter but they can also conceal. Ightham Mote in Kent must be one of the least known of historical buildings in England. It evaded Cromwell's grasp because it is concealed in a cup-shaped valley, its moat virtually redundant. Nowadays it looks like nothing so much as a religious house or an Oxford or Cambridge college, a place of serenity and calm, but they do dredge up suits of chainmail from the moat and have found a girl's body in a wall. The American military base at Molesworth similarly lies in a cup-shaped valley, hidden behind a dip in the land, its weaponry further concealed in silos.

The valley symbol is ambiguous because it denotes a certain kind of relationship with the land. Do we use it as our servant, for our own purposes, some of which can be good, or do we have it as our friend, finding ourselves in it and it in ourselves? Religious men and women in the middle ages lived out this ambiguity to the full. Those men who went into the valleys, especially wild and remote ones, in their search for God and for community unwittingly began to exploit the very environment which afforded them shelter.

For if the valley is an image of seclusion and so carries the snare of delusion or secrecy, it is also a place of richness and variety and so it carries all the snares which lead us to desire to possess and accumulate. Temptation exists in the valley just as it did in the desert. In the valley, however, it is more dangerous because it is objectified, outside ourselves. In this sense the valley can carry our projections and cradle us from reflection. It can prevent us from acknowledging what we do.

Economic factors

In the twelfth century monasticism flourished and became what we nowadays might call a growth industry. The monks took over wide tracts of land which were considered unfit for cultivation and transformed them by their labours into magnificent sheep farms or orchards. They built fine abbey churches which dominated the landscape. They became part of the agrarian economy rather than existing independently of it. Trade routes were opened up between the large cities but wove their way round the country via the monastic houses. This agricultural efficiency meant that the monks rapidly became rich and this was the cause of their eventual downfall. I remember hearing once that if the abbot of Glastonbury had married the abbess of Shaftesbury, they would have been the richest couple in England. Certainly her property was immense and she controlled resources such as the wrecking rights off the Dorset coast, some eighty miles away from her monastery. If the coffers did chance to run low, the landmarks could be neatly shifted and more booty brought ashore by night.

The skill with which these religious managed their property can be explained in terms of a very simple but far-reaching innovation by the Cistercians. They were the first to introduce *conversi* or lay brothers. While the literate professed monks worked in their libraries or bent their heads over the scriptures and the account books, simpler, ruder souls were out there in the fields, which began to spring up with jonquils certainly, but also with nice fat sheep. So successful was this system that at Rievaulx Abbey, for instance, at the time of Aelred, there were 140 monks and 600 lay brothers. The theory is excellent. No one is debarred from becoming a monk through lack of intelligence or education. The division of functions looks fine. In practice, however, none of us is sufficiently holy to live with so radical a divide. How can we value the place of the earth when we have nothing to do with it? How can we value the place of manual work without appearing to patronize those who have to do it day in day out?

When I was ten I had an account at the Somerset and Wiltshire Trustee Savings Bank. Every Thursday morning the Milk Marketing Board sent an immense lorry round the back lanes of Somerset to collect the beautiful brown eggs that my marran hens (about ten of them) had managed to lay that week. On Saturday I would join the other farmers at the bank. We lounged up against the counter to hand in our pay from the Milk Marketing Board; they in hundreds of pounds, me in shillings and pence. That part of being a farmer I managed quite well; I also enjoyed selling my pony's manure to my mother, for her roses. My little cow, Chloe, flourished too, especially when she escaped over the hedge and in the fullness of time produced a calf. That was the beginning of the end, however. My father caught brucellosis from the milk; shady dealings were negotiated at a higher level and Chloe was disposed of; I was packed off to school and my farming days came to an end.

Since that time I have lived with the divide in a way I would have thought inconceivable when I used to milk Chloe, washing down her udder, pressing my head into her warm hairy side and hearing the thin splash of milk hissing into an empty pail. My entire subsequent education and life have conspired to keep my hands and head apart. And I am not holy enough to make up the divide. Even as a novice, at a time when I worked a lot with my hands, the split was perpetuated. One of my first memories of the religious life is of arriving in the convent kitchen and being asked to break one hundred and forty-four eggs. At the end of this process there lay a nice collection of omelettes. My point is that through pressure of time, I was not invited to help make omelettes, but merely to smash eggs.

When people work so efficiently it is possible to become extremely rich and after a bit to forget to ask the obvious questions. What does it feel like to work as a cog in a wheel? What kind of attitude are you developing towards the tools of your trade, the land you farm, the people with whom you work? The valley is a potent image of the division any one of us can experience. The Cistercians introduced a split from which the religious life has yet fully to recover.

Social considerations

As an image of division the valley serves to symbolize another innovation of the twelfth century. Just as the great monastic houses imitated society by dividing the monks according to their access to formal education and producing a two-tier system, so too the development of a mercantile class was reflected by the foundation of religious houses of canons regular, such as the Augustinians and Premonstratensians. The nascent bourgeoisie who might have difficulty in being admitted to the upper echelons of the great abbeys were thus provided with an opportunity to serve God where they lived and worked, that is to say, within the 'bourgs' or towns. The religious life both mirrors and reflects social convention and religious are naive when they imagine that they automatically represent a counter-culture.

I like the difference between the notions of mirroring and reflecting. A mirror gives me a straightforward image of myself and I am so accustomed to seeing it that I no longer notice that it does in fact invert my image. I am inclined to think that what I see in the mirror is what I look like. It takes the occasional photograph to remind me that this is not the case. A reflector, on the other hand, is deliberately set at an angle and serves to give us access to information or ways of looking at things we do not ordinarily use. Often it distorts the image it receives and we have to use our own judgement to redress the balance. I believe that the religious life has a place both in mirroring and reflecting what is happening in the world as a whole. In the past we have used the word 'prophetic' rather arrogantly of the religious life. We have said that it challenges convention and have claimed almost magical properties for its reflective function. In this way we have lost touch with its simpler and humbler task of mirroring, and have prevented dialogue between religious and laity. We need each other for the right questions to be addressed. We need each other in order to have the right conversation even. We need each other for the mirror to become a lens and show us a true image rather than an inverted one.

I see this dialogue as having really significant implications when we begin to talk about the vows. In the novices' talks I have given in Chelsea I have found myself speculating out loud about the images of obedience, poverty and chastity one might receive if one were to walk out in London. Within one hundred yards of the building stands the Chelsea hospital, home for retired soldiers. Vowed obedience is so very different from military obedience. How? Why? Walking on to the river Thames and continuing east one would eventually come to 'cardboard city' where homeless people live in a shanty town of cardboard boxes underneath Charing Cross railway bridge. Most 'poor' religious people have a very different experience of poverty. How? Why? Further east still, there are places where to talk of chastity would be to talk of a luxury, the luxury of being able to choose not to go on the streets to make a living. How? Why?

Where our practice as poor, chaste and obedient people is not informed by some kind of dialogue with the world, it readily becomes naive. We 'magicalize' money, sex and power when we talk about the vows in terms of renunciation. We remove ourselves from the responsibility that comes with being as essentially middle class as most religious in Britain and Ireland are. Vowed life is God's gift to us, not our gift to God and grace builds on nature, nature on grace. People who enjoy the religious life and thrive on it are people who are right to choose this way of coming to God. It fits in with how they see themselves rather than being appended as some awful burden they are forcing themselves to carry around. Their call is no different from the one call every Christian receives at baptism, the call to be human and to be holy. The theology of the vows which informed Church practice twenty years ago saw the vows as things which people took and which effected a change within them. The change was seen as progress, a way of ensuring they were brought close to God. Nowadays we talk more readily about the vows as process, as a way of engaging with, or being in, the world. Consequently it becomes easier to say that there is not really anything as clear cut as poverty, chastity or obedience; there are only poor, chaste and obedient people who are trying to grow to God this way. Some of them happen to be professed religious; some of them happen to be married people or single people. All are engaged on a human journey whose goal is God.

This quality of journeying is reflected in another twelfth-century innovation. The Cistercians were the first religious not to allow infant oblation, or the offering of children to a monastery. Although this practice has honourable roots, and the story of the call of the infant Samuel (1 Samuel 3) remains a favourite 'call story' with many, in itself it is a strange thing to do. A child who is dedicated to a monastery or convent and reared there is not really choosing this way of coming to God. The Cistercian innovation reminds us that any choosing of a vowed life must be undertaken by someone who is sufficiently adult to be able to make some kind of commitment to engage with the forces of good and evil in this particular context. Elsewhere I have written of the tendency we have to idealize, satirize and romanticize the religious life (see *Women before God*, chapter seven). We do not allow religious to be real people who have to struggle with the same myths and problems that face everyone else. Behind the practice of infant oblation lies a sentimentalizing of the religious life, as though a certain kind of innocence were necessary in those who come to God this way. The question, 'Do you have to be a virgin to be a nun?' is one with which everyone who has addressed groups about the religious life will be familiar. A lay friend who was present when I talked to her sixth form group added the comment, 'Is that before, during or after you enter?' The corny note of realism behind her joke was very helpful. I wonder why we set such high standards for religious people. I wonder why we have a tendency to prefer to think that their story should be different from anyone else's. For women in particular some of the projections which have been put on to Mary have been put on to them as well. Just as she was conceived without original sin, so we should live without any sin. Just as she was both virgin and mother, so we should be virgins and 'spiritual mothers'. It is so hard to reclaim the feminine within God when all that it might be appropriate to name in God is transferred for safety's sake to Mary the mother of Jesus. It is hard to name all that is wounded and hurt within oneself when the Church colludes with society in wanting everything to be shiny and bright.

The practice of infant oblation was consciously abandoned by the Cistercians because the fullness of the Christian life makes very adult demands. This is true whether such fullness is sought in a monastery or in the world. Each of these constitutes a valley, a place of seclusion and of 'engagement', where this life is revealed in all its complexity.

Cultural factors

This engagement had an even sharper focus in the product of another marriage between the Church and the world. Nowadays we are inclined to regard the Crusades with detached interest. They so evidently did not work that it is hard to imagine a world in which *outremer*, the prospect of fighting overseas, had an allure which could call Europe to arms. This drive had an effect on the religious life which has since been considerably tamed. Few active religious orders would be totally at ease with the idea that they should count the Knights Templars or Knights Hospitallers among their forebears. The image is somehow not exactly congruent with how we see ourselves today. Yet the idealism which led some to take up arms on behalf of the Church led others to organize pastoral intervention of a very ordinary and simple kind. The Knights Templars offered protection to pilgrims; the Knights Hospitallers offered nursing care. Moreover the Templars introduced certain practices which were to have a long-lasting effect on the way later religious orders would organize themselves. They did not have autonomous houses as the medieval religious had done; rather they divided into regions, countries, priories and bailiwicks and used elections in order to appoint their officials. This tendency to centralize constitutes one of the main strengths of the military orders. They were actual, they responded to the needs of the times and they were structured in a way that would enable improvisation and adaptation to local conditions rather than inhibit it.

Nowadays they have vanished or, as in the case of the Hospitallers, have vestigial remains: their full name 'Hospitallers of St John of Jerusalem' is preserved by the St John's Ambulance service. In their place we have religious congregations and other organizations doing comparable work, ministering to ordinary human needs.

The tradition that developed out of the desert, mountain and valley could no longer lean exclusively upon images of withdrawal, even a withdrawal which was essentially an attempt to draw closer to God and to the cosmic forces of good and evil battling within. The next couple of centuries saw further developments already hinted at in the valley tradition and it is these that must now be examined.

5
Reclaiming the market place

❧❧❧

The market place makes an intriguing image. A market is a place of barter and exchange but it is also a place for showing off one's wares. The anonymity of present-day Stock Market exchanges, with transactions done via telephones and computer terminals, is a long way from the essentially public face of commerce on the street. The patter of the man with a suitcase full of inexpensive jewellery outside the department store on Oxford Street is nearer the mark: 'These didn't fall off the back of a lorry, darling; they were pushed.' The market place is loud and can be vulgar; it is dirty and can dirty those who work there. Like the valley, it is a place of extraordinary richness and variety; unlike the valley, it is a place where this profusion is on public display to tempt eye and hand. It is a place of exchange, a place where money is named without shame, a place where the 'haves' possess the earth and the 'have nots' scavenge in their wake.

These are the messages of the external image. However the market place exists within us as well. We are all engaged in dialogues in which we trade off bits of ourselves. Sometimes we barter and haggle over these bits, well aware of what we are doing. At other times we connive; we do not even acknowledge that we are 'shopping' our experience and identity in the name of the supposedly Christian virtues of peace and quiet.

Those who founded religious communities in the market place or used it as the forum for speaking God's message to the world inherited a tradition which had promoted isolation and withdrawal. They gave a whole new focus and force to the tradition by taking religion back to the people from whom their forebears had apparently withdrawn. Commerce too may be redeemed; even our internal commerce, barter and exchange.

Faith in the market place

The principal innovators of the thirteenth century were Francis
(1181-1226) and Dominic (1170-1221). Both were answering a
call which Francis heard articulated in the words, 'Go repair my
house which, as you see, is well-nigh in ruins.' Francis understood
this literally at first and only later came to see that the words had
some sort of general application. God's house is more than a
collection of stones and Francis progressively discovered that his
work was to be done in the city men build of stones and which
they can so easily reduce to stones. In Scripture the city has a bad
track record and is a highly ambiguous symbol. The story of the
building of the tower of Babel told in Genesis 11 is one of the
many 'fall stories' recorded in that book. To attempt to build a
ziggurat that will reach heaven is to vie with God and to lay claim
to space that God alone can give. The sacrifice of Cain, the settled
farmer who cultivates a stable plot of land in order to grow crops
from it, is rejected. That of the nomad, Abel, is accepted. The
very worst patterns of settlement are the two cities of the plain,
Sodom and Gomorrah, which refused hospitality to God's angels,
and with their fall every city is somehow discredited.

Later, however, those who wrote the Bible began to see an
image of God's place and purpose in Jerusalem, the holy city.
Here Mount Zion is watered and sustained from within: 'There is
a river whose streams refresh the city of God, and it sanctifies the
dwelling of the Most High. God is inside the city . . .' (Psalm
46.4). This is the city that Francis knew in Assisi, a prosperous
comfortable place where his father's status as a rich merchant
was destined to become his own. Only it did not work out that
way, even though grace builds on nature. It is not by accident that
the merchant's son is called to redeem the market place; the boy
called to grow to independence.

The two main innovations which we owe to Francis have an
extraordinary relevance in today's world. First, he worked out
something profound about money and, secondly, he saw the
implications of this for our everyday use of creation and power.
The most far-reaching vision given to the Church about what we
mean by poverty was elaborated in a market place. Francis's
starting point was at once his own personal experience — that
ecstatic run naked through the streets of Assisi — and the

drawing of Christ. Nowadays well-established religious congregations manage their money alongside other international corporations, and discover that it is equally subject to market forces. Nowadays the radical poverty of a Francis would be seen as imprudence or lunacy. His own brethren had to tease out the practical implications of his vision after he had died and attempt to give it a legislative shape. The present-day Franciscan way of life is their product, not his. For Francis the only rule was the life of Jesus. He wrote of his desire to 'follow in the teaching and footsteps of Our Lord Jesus Christ' and to 'observe the holy gospel of Christ'.

The experience of the early Church as recorded in the Acts of the Apostles and the letters of Paul gives two different models for the practice of poverty, and down the centuries individual Christians or Christian groups have oscillated between the two. Those who belonged to the Jerusalem church described in Acts shared their goods in common and distributed surplus to the needy. Their community found expression in justice and almsgiving. In the Pauline churches meanwhile, poverty was seen as an attitude rather than a necessary practice. People should be detached from material possessions because the world is not a permanent place; the end is nigh. Laziness and escapism were condemned by Paul because daily work is in itself a preparation for the *parousia* or second coming of the Lord.

For Francis inspiration came from the example of the Jerusalem church. He reacted against the ascetic poverty practised in the monasteries in the name of a poverty he found modelled in the life of Jesus and in the lives of his first followers. The 'poor monks, rich monasteries' option he rejected because he had heard Jesus himself describe his Church as 'well-nigh in ruins'. Francis chose the 'Lady Poverty' with all the fervour and devotion with which his contemporaries, the troubadours, sang of courtly love; the market place became the field of the cloth of gold or tweed or nice plain worsted where Francis jousted for her honour. Two centuries later, Ignatius Loyola would commend Jesuits to 'love poverty as a mother'. These maternal images speak of God the provider, a God who is concerned to give and to share and whose will it is that we do likewise. In the service of this God Francis practised the radical poverty of complete simplicity and total dependence. His model was the Jesus of the gospels and with him he found honour in the beauty of the material world — the flowers of the field which outshine Solomon in all his glory (Matthew 6.29) — brother sun, sister moon, brother wolf and sister bear. His experience of poverty led him into a new relationship with nature and all forms of natural beauty.

What does this have to say to our lives? Behind this question lies another about how we understand the 'imitation of Christ'. What do we mean by the expression 'following Jesus' or when we talk about being 'present-day disciples'? Francis spoke of following 'in the teaching and footsteps of Our Lord Jesus Christ'. Here he alludes to a favourite image from the New Testament: the disciple or *akolouthos* is the one who is on the path or *kelouthos*. This language is used principally in the synoptic gospels and notably by Mark. John, meanwhile, calls the disciple *mathetes*, the one who has been taught personally by the Lord and has absorbed this in all she or he does and says and is, through the divine indwelling. These two positions suggest either external imitation or internal imitation. They both have strengths but equally they can both lead to a place where the evangelists did not intend them to go. The first can conceal a doctrine of works and we owe to Luther the insight that *non imitatio fecit filios sed filatio fecit imitatores* (it is not imitation which makes us the sons and daughters of God, but the divine image within which enables us to imitate). The second can lead to a kind of moral imitation which ends up beyond passivity as quietism. The *mimetai* or disciples of Paul's writings, meanwhile, are those who are forgiven by God and who owe all their being to God and to this forgiveness. This was Francis's understanding and so his injunction continues, 'let us hold to the words, life, teaching and holy gospel of Christ'. Christ the risen Lord of the Christian life gives more than a pattern for our imitation, more than a set of attitudes which alter the way we think, he brings the transformation of grace which Francis knew in his own experience.

With this understanding of discipleship in mind I find myself looking again at the dialogue which is set up when Christians enter the market place. I am reminded that banking began in Jewish hands precisely because of some of the disquiet Christians have about money. This disquiet reflects a profound truth: in our own personal experience we know that money can corrupt us, none of us can cast the first stone. Equally, however, some of the anti-Semitism which still bedevils the Christian community stems from the projection tactics adopted by the medieval Church. If money corrupts, then put the control of money-lending into the hands of a community which has already been written off as corrupt, the Jews. If this sounds like parody, why do I still feel uncomfortable when I speak to school leavers in prestigious Roman Catholic boarding schools whose one desire is to become merchant bankers? The caring professions are somehow 'all right'; banking and politics, arts and the media are more questionable. Yet why should this be so? What unresolved questions about the following of Christ in the market place are concealed by my disquiet?

Why can I accept that a knife is a knife is a knife, whether used by a surgeon, a mother slicing bread or a murderer? The knife is morally neutral, the person using it is not. Why can I not so easily accept that money is money is money whether used by a single parent to buy groceries, by a financier to buy stocks and shares or by Bob Geldof to generate aid for Ethiopia? Why do I find money inherently wrong even before I begin to consider questions that relate to how I use it? One reason could be that the Christian Churches have not always addressed the question with the simplicity of a Francis. We cannot speak with his authority because we have never really been stripped of everything, let alone offered ourselves for such stripping. We have gone for the easy option of making the rich feel guilty about their money and the poor feel patronized for their lack of it. Francis's voice has authority because his practice matched his words. He was not saying that he felt uncomfortable being a material person, rather the contrary — he loved the world. His dialogue with the world exemplified by the market place seems to be saying that we need not be afraid either of poverty or of riches. What matters is that we examine our images of failure and of success and assess the extent to which we judge people according to their means. Our value judgements are too easily based upon appearances. Like Jesse we imagine that the older brothers are necessarily better than younger brothers, while God looks to the shepherd boy to become king. The story of the anointing of David contains the reminder that 'Human beings look at appearances but Yahweh looks at the heart' (1 Samuel 16.7).

In a market economy images of success and images of failure

are put under real pressure. Do we secretly assume that rich people are better than poor people? Is this why we all seek to get rich, or at least to have rich friends and patrons? These are the images Francis can help us revisit and analyse. His message has 'street-cred' because he worked it out on the street but it is a message which belongs to an older version of the tradition as well. In his first letter John wrote, 'It is not every spirit that you can trust; test them to see if they come from God. You can tell the spirits that come from God by this: every spirit which acknowledges that Jesus the Christ has come in the flesh is from God' (1 John 4.1-2). To know Jesus in the flesh is to acknowledge the material order and yet to seek Jesus within it. Our problem is that we too readily seek ourselves within it and end up judging our own worth, not to mention the worth of other people, according to how much we have. We then begin to feel guilty about this, turn on the flesh, and deny and denigrate it in the name of humility. We lack the vision of faith or what Karl Barth saw when he talked about the poverty which is the 'obedience of faith'. The obedience of faith is a discipline, a whole new way of looking at the world and being in the world. It commits us to a non-possessive relationship with the material order, and to chaste relationships with our brothers and sisters, the moon, the sun and the stars. What I believe Francis's story illustrates is that visions are valid and that we need the lunacy of an extremist to remind us of our own deepest ideals. Moreover we need this faith to be displayed in the market place almost more than anywhere else. For in the market place the commercial or trade-based nature of our interpersonal exchanges is laid bare. Whenever we talk, treat or deal with other people, we are the very currency of our own exchanges. If God is not to be sought in these, God cannot really be sought anywhere.

For this reason I am not surprised when I notice that Francis first began to preach while still a layman. His authority came from his experience and it was given shape and substance when Pope Innocent III approved the first small group of twelve Franciscans who had gathered together by the year 1210. They were to preach and to live on alms. In time they developed a system of what today we would call 'outreach', perfectly adapted to their times. This was the Third Order, a way in which lay people could share the vision and begin themselves to off-load some of their own false security and engage with real questions about Christian trading. Just as the guilds were developed for commercial reasons, to enable entrepreneurs to organize themselves and their market, so too a new spirituality enabled them to make Christian sense of what they were doing. Lay spirituality was an obvious development in the late middle ages because the Scriptures began to circulate in the vernacular and people could read the gospel stories for themselves in their own homes. The Franciscan Third Order gave them a framework within which to do this reading. They could learn that Jesus's friends included Matthew the tax gatherer and Judas who kept the common purse: the lay man who was up-front about barter and exchange, the religious man who was not.

The university world

Another area of life in need of a theological and spiritual framework was that of the universities. They sit somewhat uneasily alongside the market place yet both are city institutions and have lessons for each other. The university church, Great St Mary's, in Cambridge represents this nicely. One side is set looking towards King's College chapel and the most beautiful views in Cambridge, the other stands over the market square and is even nowadays surrounded by jaunty canvas-topped stalls on market day. Andy's Records and the cheese stall are an inescapable fact of life in Cambridge. The market belongs because it is a reminder that in universities too there is barter, albeit at the level of ideas. And these can also be stolen, traded and exploited, just as much as the rich stuff of material wealth.

The church which Dominic found to be 'well-nigh in ruins' was equally uneasily placed. It was the church of southern France rocked by the Albigensian heresy, a church in need of intelligent learning and the eloquence that could take this learning out on to the street. Dominic had already been a canon at Osma cathedral in Spain before beginning his travels and had followed the rule of St Augustine there. Where Francis began his active life as a layman, Dominic was already a scholar and a priest. Once again his natural gifts fitted him for the work he had to do. He moved easily in a world where a university education could be obtained in Paris, Toulouse, Bologna or Rome. His order was approved only six years after that of Francis, in 1216.

Dominic's chief innovation still has lessons for groups and communities today. He set up a very careful system of checks and balances which would enable legislative and executive functions to be operated by the same group of people when they met for consultation in chapter. In this I find a way of looking at power which intrigues me. Benedict separated tasks for efficiency's sake. Dominic brings functions together in a context where everyone in the community can talk to each other by acknowledging each other and recognizing each other's existence. In our everyday dealings we are inclined either to magicalize people by attributing too much power to them — bosses, union leaders, politicians, judges, police — or to be afraid of people because they appear to represent chaos — striking miners, punks, yuppies. Harmony can be achieved not by setting up barriers between us and other people but by bringing everyone in the community together in a single forum. Then exploitation becomes more difficult, trading more likely to be just, and barter a public face, for a true exchange is both sanctioned and preserved.

If this is true in the public world, how much more true is it in the world of our private lives. We too readily divide our own personalities. First, there are the nice orderly bits we know our way around and which we are happy to allow to control whatever happens to us by letting them legislate for every eventuality. Then there are the frightening, scary bits which represent chaos and should only be allowed to execute orders delivered from above. Dominic's vision would allow us to set up conversations between the two. I have seen this so clearly in dreams but too easily lack the courage to set up this exchange in everyday life. A prayer exercise I have been given while on retreat has however helped me see what might happen. I was invited to sit with my weak left hand holding my right strong hand, cradling and supporting it and taking its full weight. Then I reversed the process and listened to what my body was trying to tell me. I began to see that I need my weak self to care for my strong self; that the chaos I fear is a vain fantasy; that the dialogue is mutually beneficial because it reveals the intentions of each. In this dialogue I am not asked to trade off bits of myself, nor sacrifice them to each other, but only to own the rights and needs of each.

If Francis had one half of the insight, that poverty is not

49

something to be afraid of, then in Dominic I find a way of letting this insight be operative in my own personal life. A week ago I sat on the ground and tinkered with my moped. I got cold and grubby and had smears of oil all over my face and hands. A year ago at a time of unease and disquiet, I put my head on the ground, burying my face in the pile of a circular rug and prayed in silence. Six months before that I sailed over to Ireland on the Friday night ferry through a raging March sea. I felt quite terrified of the violence of the waves and the lurching ship until I lay on the ground in a gangway. There I allowed my body to be carried and rocked by the sea. I suddenly saw that this stretch of sea belongs to all the waters over the face of the earth and felt myself drawn into them and cradled by them. Each of these pictures describes a moment when an experience of childishness, weakness or fear brought me to insight. These are moments Francis risked meeting when he stripped himself of material possessions in the market place. They are moments Dominic enables me to enjoy because he sets up a way for me to do it. He organized a dialogue which would allow the weak and the strong to speak to each other when he legislated for consultation between the two at every level of his order's conventual deliberations.

Armed with the insights of these two men I find it possible to seek a vision of Christian presence in the city which is neither fundamentalist nor triumphalist, neither condemnatory nor reproachful. It is a form of Christian presence which sets up a conversation with the world of commerce where the poor, the weak and the displaced have a voice. It is a form of Christian presence which, with Francis, knows it is all right to be poor and, with Dominic, says, 'so listen to this'. The rich man was condemned not because he was rich, but because he ignored the poor man, Lazarus, who lay at his gate covered with sores (Luke 16.19–31).

6

Contemplating the universe

✤✤✤

The vision that began in the desert, extended onto the mountain, visited the valley and redeemed the city eventually broke loose from these localized sites and embraced the whole world. Where the founders of the orders that began in each of these contexts were the product of their times and children of their age, Ignatius Loyola (1491–1556), was heir to the tradition they had spent fifteen hundred years elaborating. To Pachomius he owed insights into the centrality of discernment; to Benedict the place of community and flexibility; to the Carthusians the value of excellence and spiritual ways of coming to personal holiness; to the Cistercians the wisdom that it is imprudent to legislate for success by setting up a total system; to the Canons Regular the awareness that a marriage of monastic and apostolic practices can be uneasy; to the Knights Templars and Hospitallers the place of variety and lure of the Holy Land; to Francis the value of real poverty and to Dominic the value of academic learning.

I believe this to be one reason why Ignatian spirituality is enjoying such popularity at the moment. It is a spirituality which enables people to integrate and own all the influences that have fed into the development of their personal story. It is a spirituality which enables you to live in the world as the woman or man that you are and to seek and find God alone in all the formative influences which constitute your own context. It is a spirituality of the universe within and the universe without.

Ignatius and the apostolic religious life
With Ignatius the form of religious life which has contributed most to the building of the kingdom of God in this world through the work of apostolic men and women was first fully developed.

51

This is the unenclosed active religious life, that of people who are available to serve the world because the world is the place where they live and move and have their being.

He left two formative texts to the Church, the *Spiritual Exercises* and the *Constitutions of the Society of Jesus*. Both contain not just a description of what we might do in God's service in the world or even why we might do it but a way of arriving at understanding how we are to do God's work. His is a mysticism of service. His *Spiritual Exercises* are now available to lay people and religious alike in a way that was inconceivable some twenty years ago, in retreats that can be made either in retreat houses or in one's own home. The *Constitutions of the Society of Jesus* remain less accessible, yet they contain a pattern which can help people to go on being influenced by the *Exercises*. They are as much a charter for living an actively contemplative, or contemplatively active, life in the world as the *Exercises* are. In this chapter I want to look at the *Exercises* and the *Constitutions* in the conviction that both texts furnish the individual Christian — and Christian groups — with a way of seeking and finding God's will in the events, people and situations of everyday living. Both the universe within and the universe without may be constellated to God's 'greater glory'. Ignatius the star-gazer invites us to become part of the moving dust of the universe, a dust which can dream.

The 'Spiritual Exercises'

I do not really understand the instructions manual for my moped. For a start it is written in something called Eurospeak, that is to say in a mixed collection of European languages. The translations are terrible and it does not inspire my confidence to find my poor little bike referred to throughout as a mopped. At the moped shop where I take it to be maintained, however, the engineer is in a totally different position. He ignores the manual when I try to hand it to him. He turns on the engine, listens to it running and then pronounces his diagnosis. I envy him his powers of discernment and his expertise. But then I do have to concede that he is an experienced mechanic, he knows his job and does not have to consult the pictures in the little book to know what the choke looks like.

The book of the *Spiritual Exercises* is similar to my moped manual. It is written in shorthand and has suffered over the years from some poor translations. A translator is always tempted to interpret and Ignatius has been ill served by some of his interpreters. It is a book for specialists to use and the best of these specialists, like my moped mechanic, will in fact not be working with the book in one hand. They will have internalized the text and learnt how to apply its dynamics to the needs of the individual woman or man with whom they are in what I choose to call the 'retreat-conversation'. This conversation is conducted in interviews — one a day during a closed retreat in a retreat house, one a week or fortnight in other adapted forms of making the *Exercises*, outside a closed, silent retreat house. There are more instructions for the way the retreat director is to conduct these interviews than for any other single activity during the retreat. The director is to be brief in presenting the material with which the retreatant is invited to pray, for the real work of the retreat is done by the retreatant alone with God. Some of these prayer exercises relate to the Scriptures, since during the thirty days of the retreat the one making the *Exercises* is going to be praying with the story of the life, death and resurrection of Jesus. The text of others is written out in detail by Ignatius, for he has a clear pattern and plan for the conduct of the retreat. He has an insight into where retreatants are coming from and where they might want to move to. The only real task of the one who gives the *Exercises* is to help retreatants locate this pattern in their own lives.

The pattern is of God drawing near with a call, made known to us in the only word God has ever spoken, that is to say in Jesus. The call will be revealed to women and men who listen to the voice of the Spirit as they begin to talk and listen to the universe of their own relationships and feelings and reactions. This is a spirituality of intimacy: intimacy with God, with oneself and with the world. The exercises of the first week envisaged by Ignatius have an extraordinary brief: to see what stands in the way of this intimacy. Consequently they do not operate at the level of ideas — because any of us can say what our ideas about God are. Rather they visit our fears about what God might be like. They visit our memories and trawl through our own experience to see what our operative theology is. Inside each of us there lurks an image of ourselves and of God which is likely to have been damaged by our experience of neglect, pain, weakness or dread. These images too can safely be taken out and looked at in the light of love. And then we come to understand what sin is and what God is doing when we are offered salvation, forgiveness and healing. I, as I really am, am loved by a God whom I have not known because I have chosen to fear God and hide from God in the garden of my own shame.

Ignatius uses a fascinating procedure to enable this insight to surface in the understanding of the individual retreatant. He invites us to consider first the sin of the angels from the mythological beginnings of salvation history, secondly the sin of Adam and of Eve, thirdly that of some person who might be in hell, and finally to move on to consider our own sins. By projecting our fears we are able to own the violence, pride and deceit we all bear within. First we objectify it, by calling it the sin of someone else. Then we can know it and name it at work in our own lives. This is only possible because God is revealed as the compassionate one who desires that we choose life and not the death of living with our lies.

Throughout the first week of the *Exercises* Ignatius invites me both to look at the place of sin in forming my understanding of myself and of God and also to look at my feelings and reactions. He begins to teach me something which will only become fully important to me in the later weeks of the retreat. He helps me see that I have a set of understandings inside me which he calls 'Rules for the Discernment of Spirits'. I arrive at the retreat with these rules and during the retreat I am invited to see that some of them are harmful to me. Because I associate feeling good with being good and feeling bad with being bad, I may have failed to notice that negative feelings can in fact help me to grow towards God. Likewise I may not have noticed that there is often a feeling of disappointment or depression lurking after I have followed one of my more inspired and impulsive decisions. Ignatius's 'Rules for the Discernment of Spirits', which he offers as a corrective, are arguably his greatest gift to the Church and the most abiding legacy for any one who makes the *Exercises*. During the last two weeks of the retreat I am invited to continue to experience the difference between equating good feelings with the call of God and bad feelings with the call of the evil one as I follow Jesus towards his death and being raised from the dead. When I pray with the passion story I am led to face a central truth of

Christianity about the place of pain and of the testing that death brings to all our bright hopes and aspirations.

In this way the rest of my life will be available to me to live in the spirit of the final text of the *Exercises*, the 'Contemplation to Attain Love'. In this exercise Ignatius reveals the harmony that is there for us to perceive in the ordering of all things, including dreams, desires and failure. The God who is 'above all things' is a God who desires to give me everything, who is constantly giving me everything and inviting me to seek and find the Giver in every gift. Ignatius does not use this title for God, but talks of the Divine Majesty, a name familiar to those who have prayed with Cranmer's Prayer Book of 1662. In this as in much else Ignatius shows himself to be one of the Reformers. Certainly in teaching people discernment by means of his Rules, he was empowering individuals in a way the centralizing Church of his day found quite threatening. He was enabling them to see the place of glory and the quest for God's glory but equally the place of pain and disappointment. For the will of God may be discerned in all our feelings and not just in some of them; God's will for the outer universe is waiting to be discerned in our inner universe, in our innermost selves.

The *Spiritual Exercises* are also something of a school of prayer and Ignatius proposes a variety of prayer methods to the one who makes them. He uses words like meditation and contemplation in a specialized way and encourages the retreatant to learn by doing. When I meditate with passages from Scripture according to Ignatius's method I am, as it were, a spectator. I watch the Jesus who is at work in the gospel stories and my heart is warmed by the words he speaks to me, 'Your faith has made you whole, go in peace' (Mark 5.34), 'Go and do likewise' (Luke 10.37), 'Blessed are the meek' (Matthew 5.5), 'Today I will dwell in your house' (Luke 19.5). When I contemplate the Scriptures according to his method I become a participant in the gospel stories. My imagination is the greatest God-given tool I bring to this task, for with my imagination I begin a dialogue with the gospel text. All the energy of my unconscious becomes available to me as I pray my story with the story of Jesus. It is not just that my sins are forgiven; more than this, I am able to see what my sins are. I learn that I am far more tempted to choose the death of fear and denial than the life-giving and costly forces of love. I learn with Catherine of Siena that 'God does not ask a perfect work, but infinite desire'. I learn that the contexts in which the healing and calling word of Jesus is addressed to me are where I lead my everyday life. He is not safely concealed in a time warp; he is here and now walking the streets I know and sitting down at every table at which I eat. His universe begins to invade my universe and I can contemplate him there. In Gerard Manley Hopkins's words, 'Down all that glory in the heavens to glean our Saviour' ('Hurrahing in Harvest').

How does the person who has made the *Spiritual Exercises* pray in ordinary life after the retreat or even fit back into ordinary life? When I finished making the *Exercises* I felt like an apple that had been peeled. The peeling had been gently and carefully done but I emerged feeling almost unnaturally sensitive. With the passing of time however, this changed and I found that I felt sensitized, increasingly aware of what was happening inside me and of the difference this was making to the life I live in the outer world. I am not saying that I went off and started preaching the gospel of social reform, that I changed my life-style to become more like that of the poor, or that I made any major life decisions. Rather I have noticed that over the years this experience of having made the full Ignatian *Exercises* has given me the desire to seek and find God in the real relationships I have with the people I know and love and the people I know and find difficult. Over and above that I have been presented with a context in which a question of justice does demand my attention and I am increasingly called to opt for the poverty of identifying with a group of poor people who lie uncomfortably close to my own back door. They actually inhabit my very home; I am learning to talk to them and invite them to share their sense of pain and isolation with me. These characters are the poor and weak I find within myself; they make up my poor and weak self. Moreover this dialogue is beginning to affect the way I relate to the poor and weak in the outer world. It has given real force and form to the work I do with other people, notably other women, helping me identify this weakness wherever I meet it. This is increasingly involving me in questions of justice because I am learning to ask the question 'Why?' of the injustice I inflict upon myself and see inflicted on others. I am beginning to recognize the insecurity that leads us into power games and into oppression, the hierarchies that bedevil our thinking and consequently our relationships.

The place of the Ignatian 'Constitutions'

Ignatius provides me with a further context. He enables me to carry the insights of the *Spiritual Exercises* out into the world of everyday living which constitutes my universe. From the *Constitutions* I learn that his *Spiritual Exercises* belong to a wider framework of formation. They are the first of a series of six experiences which are intended to train Jesuits. In each of the other experiences or 'Experiments' as they are called, the fledgling Jesuit works for a month or so in an unfamiliar context and tests the extent to which the insights of the retreat are deepened by this work. The experiments he proposes have their twentieth-century equivalents; each of us can in fact find similar contexts without having to do anything too dramatic. What matters is not the 'Where?' of each experiment but the 'Why?'. Why does he send his young men to serve in hospitals, to make a pilgrimage without money, begging from door to door, to work within their own houses in 'various lowly and humble offices', to explain Christian doctrine to 'boys and other simple persons' and to preach or hear confessions?

The answer, I believe, is that in each of these situations, the young men in question — who have been selected for their excellence, their intelligence and good health, even for their good looks — will meet aspects of themselves and of their universe which otherwise they might be tempted to avoid or to ignore. In a hospital one meets sickness and despair, the poverty of dependence and the reversals by which the strong become weak. I have such a strong memory of a big, golden-headed forty-year-old lorry-driver dying of cancer. He joined in with the carol singers when they came round and my throat tightened with tears as he sang 'O little town of Bethlehem' with its line about the 'dear Christ' who may 'enter in'. I believe that I had been sent to work in the hospice to see this particular dying man. On pilgrimage one meets other kinds of poverty: one's own limited strength and resources and hitherto unknown fears and phobias — of the dark, of sudden noises, of strangers or strange behaviour. When knocking on the door of other people's homes one meets the domestic universe of strangers, contexts which are far removed from the nice clean homes which ordinarily produce vocations to the religious life. During the daytime these homes are the place where women are working and the next experiment revisits this insight by affording the young men the opportunity to do comparable work. In exercising themselves around the house in 'humble offices' they are in effect doing housework. They are learning what it feels like to be the one who stays at home and does the chores, the one whose universe is circumscribed by domestic concerns, the one who is rarely thanked.

The unlettered and the boys to whom Ignatius next directs his novices also represent elements of a shadow which they might otherwise choose to ignore. If their further professional training will equip them to work in the corridors of power, it is essential that they should not be ignorant of ignorance. Otherwise they might be tempted to despise it and dismiss the ignorant out of hand. They might forget that there are other qualities and capacities in the human heart which in their own intelligence they lack. For this reason too they are to preach, and hear confessions if they are priests, for in taking on a pastoral role they will be exposed to universal pain and to the real concerns we all seek to bring to God.

Ignatius's *Constitutions* are a formation document, for each of the ten sections demonstrates how individual Jesuits are to be incorporated into the body of the Society of Jesus and then, once they belong there, how they are to be that body in the world. The missionary purpose both of the text and of Ignatius's whole venture is revealed when Jerome Nadal, one of his earliest companions, wrote in 1554, 'It should be noted that in the Society of Jesus there are different kinds of houses or dwellings. These are the house of probation, the college, the professed house and the journey and by this last the whole world becomes our house.' The barriers between the domestic world and the rest of the universe are raised when people know themselves and have learnt their way round the universe within. Then they may make the whole world their universe. In this sense they have learnt the great lessons of formation; they have learnt to know that God may be sought in all things, in sickness as in health, in strangeness as in the familiar, in women and women's work as well as in men and theirs, in ignorant people as in the intelligent, in people who are in trouble as in those for whom the way seems easy. By exposure to weakness they are invited to discover the weakness that lies within and not to back off from it in shame and fear, for they are helped to see that God is in the weakness too and that the Jesus whom they met in the *Spiritual Exercises* is the one whose standard is the cross.

This Jesus enables us all to find contexts in the circumstances that constitute our universe where we may discover that God is not afraid of pain; rather it is we who read it as failure and humiliation — weakness draws God on. God's universe is peopled by 'some who are white, some black; some at peace, some at war; some weeping, some laughing; some well, some sick; some coming into the world, some dying' (*Spiritual Exercises,* n. 106) and the Incarnation, as Ignatius saw, is addressed to a universe constellated in this way.

7

The place of the home

✿✿✿

Our place in the universe has a domestic face. Each of us needs that centre we call our home, where a named space is ours by right and we do not have to earn it. It is a place where we are free to be weak and free to be strong, a place where the decisions we take — whether alone or with others — will have an immediate effect on our environment, a place where our heart is somehow at rest. On the front cover of this book is a picture of a young woman in her own home. Her name was Mary Ward and the picture was painted after she died, a considerable time after the event it attempts to depict. Her inner self contained all the elements I have tried to explore in writing about the desert and mountain, the valley, market place and universe. She faced the fear of evil, the need for companionship, the richness of variety and decisions about which bits of her self-understanding and vision to trade and which bits to give away; she knew about the universe of deep longings she carried within and the missionary zeal with which they led her to engage with the world. Above all, however, she had a quite extraordinary sense of the value of the domestic universe in which the feminine comes into its own. It is in the home that we enter into relationships, that our projections are turned round upon themselves and we learn who we are in a specific context, with definite friends in named situations.

Mary Ward's story

In the case of each of the founders of religious congregations I have mentioned so far there has been no real need to tell the story of their lives. Their stories form part of the Christian culture in which most of us have been raised. Benedict, Francis and Ignatius are household names; books about them are generally available. The story of the women founders has been veiled in much more secrecy, especially when their desire to do something new in the Church has led them into conflict with authority and the prevailing values by which the Church organized itself. Mary Ward was born in 1585 and died in 1645 in a Yorkshire that was torn by religious and civil strife. As a young woman of twenty-four she understood that she was to do something new in the Church and gathered companions about her. The picture of her in prayer before a candle contains elements which allude to this new thing — the apostolic religious life for women. In her own times she sought to give a definite public face to this venture by founding a religious community which would 'take the same as the Society of Jesus'; in our times her vision is available to be shared, interpreted and explored by women anywhere. Its lessons are valuable for men as well, as I have discovered when speaking about her to mixed groups.

The vision is depicted for us in five details of this painting. Firstly she is shown alone, and yet alone in the presence of God. As a Christian and member of a particular faith community, in her case the Roman Catholic Church, she belongs to a universal Church. This is part of her identity and a part she can take for granted. To pray however, she does not need to be in church nor for her access to God to be mediated by priest, husband or sacrament. Women may come to God as they are and in the context of their own homes at that. Domestic space is God-space for the Christbearing woman.

A second detail is revealed by the open bedchamber beside her. This is an image of her own inner space, a place where she has a body and can experience her need to return to the womb of sleep. The bedcover is blue, the colour iconography uses to hint at the divine, for 'The Lord gives to his beloved' at her most vulnerable, 'in slumber' (Psalm 127.2). Domestic space, or the home, is an image or mirror of inner space; people who feel strong within can change the environment around them. In this sense women are not doomed to stereotypic roles within the home. Where they feel personally strong and self-assured they can change the quality of the space in which they live and work by domesticizing it, that is to say by containing it as a place for relationships.

Mary Ward is shown with two books, each of which is an image of her hopes and desires. The first, in her lap, is the Bible. Again a point is being made; women can have direct access to the

Scriptures, they do not have to have the Bible mediated to them by men. Hers was a world in which women increasingly could learn Latin and thereby both read and pray with the Scriptures even before these became available in the vernacular. Where women pray with the Bible they meet Jesus the friend of women, they meet the strong women of the Old Testament tradition such as Deborah and Esther, and above all they meet a God whose image transcends gender-specific categories: the mother who forms us in the womb (Jeremiah 1.5), the watcher, the holy one who comes down from heaven (Daniel 4.23), the one who gives abundant food and fine wine (Isaiah 23.18), and who calls Judith the 'exultation of Jerusalem, the great glory of Israel, the great pride of our nation' (Judith 15.9). The second book I take to be the *Spiritual Exercises* of Ignatius because in making these *Exercises* Mary Ward had first learnt to become a discerning woman and open to God's healing call. For this reason she is not holding the book in her hands; it has led her to the Scriptures and has not become a substitute for them. It has led her to be open to the God who is depicted in the light cast by the candle and the shadow it generates.

In each of the paintings in the series of fifty-five from which this canvas comes, light and windows, candles and the sky have a dramatic role in the story line. Windows ordinarily represent choices, each of which is lit by the possibility that she may indeed find God's will and her own true self in whatever that option represents. In this picture there are two windows, her choice has narrowed from that of previous canvases in which three possibilities lay open to her. In those pictures she could choose either marriage or the monastic life or this strange and essentially new venture — the unenclosed religious life for women. The real source of life is the candle which both illumines her and casts a dark patch of shadow about her. This fifth detail — a representation of the place where light meets dark — is, I believe, a key to clarifying Mary Ward's contribution to our present-day self-understanding.

Where light meets dark
In 1617 Mary Ward said:

There is no such difference between men and women that

women may not do great things. And I hope in God it will be seen that women in time to come will do much . . . Heretofore we have been told by men we must believe. It is true we must, but let us be wise, and know what we are to believe and what not, and not to be made to think that we can do nothing. If women were made so inferior to men in all things, why were they not exempted in all things, as they are in some? . . . I would to God that all men understood this verity, that women, if they will, may be perfect, and if they would not make us believe we can do nothing, and that we are but women, we might do great matters. There was a father that lately came into England whom I heard say that he would not for a thousand of worlds be a woman, because he thought a woman could not apprehend God. I answered nothing, but only smiled, although I could have answered him, by the experience I have of the contrary. I could have been sorry for his want of judgement. I mean not to condemn his want of judgement, for he is a man of very good judgement; his want is in experience. (Quoted in *Mary Ward: a Pilgrim finds her Way*, Lavinia Byrne (Avila Press, Dublin, 1984), pp. 42–43.)

In this text I find a written account of the same dialogue that is depicted pictorially by the candlelight as it casts a shadow at Mary Ward's feet. I am not claiming that she necessarily understood that this interplay of light and dark and the conflict between them was her place within the tradition; I doubt if she saw herself in these terms. What I am saying, however, is that I believe that we can look on her story with twentieth-century hindsight and see it doing just that. Why was the reaction against her so strong? What fears did she arouse in men? Why did the Church find it necessary to imprison her at one point? In itself her vision was not that startling; it was a logical development of the continuing relationship by which the world and the Church feed insights to each other. It was inevitable that somewhere along the line a woman or group of women would want to found an order for unenclosed women, and seek the same kinds of freedom that the Jesuit fathers enjoyed, such as freedom from the restrictions of saying office together in choir and freedom from the need to wear a distinctive kind of dress. It was inevitable too that women would eventually come together in community on their own terms, that is with their own organizational structure, a woman general superior and women superiors working with her at province and local community level. For this reason, too, I believe, twentieth-century followers of her first critics disarm Mary Ward when they try to make her anodyne without examining why her contemporaries reacted so strongly against her. They thought she was toxic. Why? How? And what energies are concealed in this conflict?

In 1622 three priests, Fathers Harrison, Sherwood and Kellison wrote to Rome that Mary Ward and her first companions, 'Do not conform to feminine modesty'. They went on:

> The English Ladies conform themselves to the ways of seculars. They are idle and talkative. They speak at meetings on spiritual matters, even in the presence of priests, and give exhortations, to which they are trained in their noviceship. After they have gained entrance into titled families they teach the catechism even to men, instructing them to make acts of contrition, meditation and other spiritual practices. They gad about in town and country. It sometimes happens that they are together with men alone; they even associate with bad characters. They allow their pupils to act plays and to speak in public. They gad about in order to attract young women to enter with them. The English Ladies despite their absence of enclosure and their unmonastic way of life wish to be regarded as an order and give themselves out as such. They want to be religious but not monastic. They boast of their freedom from enclosure. They are not solidly established financially. They cannot, like other convents, live on the interest of the members' dowries. They work . . . like priests. (Quoted in *Mary Ward: a Pilgrim finds her Way*, Lavinia Byrne, pp. 24–25.)

This is the raw material of the conflict between Mary Ward and her contemporaries; it is material that is with us still and it will remain raw where its constitutive elements are not examined. All these elements are here. Firstly there is sexual stereotyping — in both its negative and positive aspects. The negative aspects are revealed where the English Ladies are accused of being 'idle and talkative' or of acting out of role by 'speaking at meetings' and encouraging their girl pupils to 'speak in public'. This is behaviour unbefitting their sex. Equally their attitude to enclosure is questioned, both because they 'gad about' and enjoy their freedom and because they have access to men, and sometimes even to 'men alone'. The message is clear; women gossip, they have a definite place in the world and should not move out of it, they should keep silence in public and are in any case a source of uneasy temptation to men. These are attitudes that still rumble on in much of the controversy that surrounds the position of women in today's Church. The debate has a different focus now; it seems to be to do with questions about the ordination of women or the 'proper' place of the contribution represented by the domestic to all our Christian thinking. In fact it is about what happens when the dark and the light start talking to each other and find that they need each other.

I wonder if this is what I mean by talking about a positive aspect of sexual stereotyping? It could be that the conflict which ranged Harrison, Sherwood, Kellison and others against Mary Ward has a clarifying aspect to it. It shows exactly what starts to happen when so-called 'masculine' qualities are claimed exclusively by men and 'feminine' qualities are heaped onto women. The presence of the dark and the light within each one of us is denied by this particular line of argument. Just because, for men, feminine qualities are frequently part of an unknown aspect of themselves and so part of the dark they may fear within, it does not mean that these qualities are to be despised wherever they are encountered. Just because, for women, masculine qualities are frequently undeveloped and so part of a dark which is feared within, it does not mean that they should all be projected out onto men who are thereby imprisoned in role. All the energy directed against Mary Ward came from a positive source, from good, if misguided, people who were genuinely seeking God's will and the good of the Church. I find this an alarming thought. It reminds me of situations I know from nowadays where the same conflict rages and is fed from the same sources of energy.

Where Mary Ward was denied access to a legitimate form of development, other women are denied the same access nowadays. Men too are caught in the same net of oppression. Neither feminine nor masculine qualities are the preserve of either sex; and feminine qualities are always set to be the losers in the power games that ensue from our sexual stereotyping.

Hence my desire to develop the image of the home as a place

for men to move into and women to move out from. The home is not a person, and so it does not carry the same gender-specific scripts. It is place we all have to make; it does not arrive out of the sky already set up. Religious communities of men and religious communities of women face the same task as any family when they seek to create a domestic setting in which to come to maturity. This raises questions about life style and the environment in which we do our home living. It is not just men who make the mistakes. I have been in women's religious houses where discomfort and clutter win the day. I have been in men's religious houses where there is a sense of space and ease any family would envy. However, the home as image is about more than this. It is about the freedom we all seek, the freedom to move around comfortably within our relationships. Domestic space is the place where light and darkness meet, and so the home is about our access to relationships and the ease we feel with them.

This morning in Regent's Park I saw a jogger dancing with his own elongated shadow as he ran round the borders of the boating lake. The February sun hangs low in the sky as I write; this morning it gave him a twenty-foot long, skinny, athletic-looking version of himself into which he could run and jump, or which he could avoid by turning sidewards and reducing it to a fearsome little gnome. He ran on and was laughing as he ran. With the sun warming his shoulders, the game was safe. This is a game we are all called to play sooner or later. There comes a time when all the 'un-ownable' parts of ourselves which have been safely projected out onto people or objects have to be taken inside and the source of our fear found within. The masculine/feminine dilemma is an obvious instance and one that is well illustrated in terms of the controversy that surrounded the life of Mary Ward. But there are others too. Our fear of pain, ill-health and the emptiness of poverty, our fear of chaos, injustice or failure all have to be met. And the place where this meeting is best done is the place where the darkness meets the light.

The place of relationships

This is the domestic space I find that Mary Ward invites me to visit. In the picture I have chosen to illustrate this idea she is shown alone. Her personal experience, however, was of companionship. We know the names of her close friends: Barbara Babthorpe, Winifred Wigmore and Mary Poyntz, Roger Lee and John Gerard, Bishop Blaise of St Omer and the Archduchess Isabella of Austria. She was a safe friend to these people, knowing which bits of her life belonged to them and which bits to herself. She did not use friendship, she gave it and received it because she had learnt her way round relationships.

In the previous chapter I suggested that Ignatius trained his men by exposing them to themselves in certain situations which would uncover their deepest hopes and fears. In this way they could learn that God does not have the same problem with failure and human weakness that we seem to have. In Mary Ward's story I find it possible to see how she made a comparable journey. The painful elements came, however, not by exposure to the fear or wickedness of unknown people, strangers who were not her kith and kin. Her pain came to her in the domestic context; she met the darkness at close quarters. It had her aunt's name when she was a child, her sister's name as she grew up and her companion Praxedes's name as her vision began to take shape. It had the Church's name as she grew older.

This experience is, I believe, shared by many women. The place where most of our learning is done is that of interpersonal relationships, with friends, lovers, husbands and children, within our own communities. We learn the place of 'give' very easily; we are not so good at the place of 'take'. Many of the scripts we carry round seem to contradict the easier ones with which God invites us to occupy our domestic space. I am not saying that it is easy space to be inside, just that the gospels are about people and the Church is about people. The gospels are very good at knowing this, the Church is less so. The ordinary human beings we meet in the stories of Jesus frequently come in pairs: the rich man and the poor man; the Pharisee and the publican; the elder brother and the profligate. There are other pairs too in the life experience of Jesus: he meets Martha and Mary; the woman with the haemorrhage and the dying child; among his friends he counts a beloved disciple and one who betrays him; he dies in the presence of a good thief and a blaspheming one. Something is being said here about the ways in which he stood, and eventually was prepared to hang, at the place where darkness and light meet, and how he tried to draw the attention of his followers to the ambiguity we all carry round and must face in our friendships, and with those we love.

The Church should also be a place where we can talk about our ambiguity. All too often it is not. At its best, liturgical celebration should be the context where this naming is done, in the presence of the community of believers gathered together to celebrate what were known as 'the Mysteries of our Redemption' when I was a child. Where we cannot speak about ambiguity in church we soon become incapable of speaking about sin as well. In present-day liturgical practice our sense of sin is easily undermined; our attempts to deal a death blow to guilt and to develop a social understanding of sin, rather than a personal one, have in many cases taken away what was good in earlier practice. The good Christian has become the endlessly cheerful one, rather than the uncertain, devout and frequently neurotic seeker we used to recognize and celebrate in the saints. What has happened inside church buildings is also happening in the wider community of Christianity. We seem concerned to present a well-scrubbed version of ourselves to the world; the profile of the good practising believer is that he or she is white, middle class, married or at least keen to become so, and so on. It is extraordinary that sinners are no longer welcome.

What has happened instead is that we have projected all the evil that belongs to ourselves out onto the world which, in consequence, becomes a wicked and terrible place. Some reclaiming of our own sinfulness has surely to be done to find harmony again and return to the balance represented by the gospels. The Church is a place where I need to know I belong because I am wicked and sinful, not in spite of it. In this way I can also face looking at the tensions and ambiguities that exist within me and know that they too can be redeemed. The Church is natural domestic space for people who are seeking God; it is the home where the halt and the lame belong. Mary Ward protested, 'I am and always have been a true daughter of holy Church' and continued to act out of her conviction that God was calling her to do something quite new. She spoke consciously as a woman, as a sinner and as someone who knew about the place where the light casts its own darkness. She had learnt the lessons of both by retaining the freedom to rest in that place.

8

A context for holding: chastity

❦

If relationships are that central, if they are where we learn who we are and how we are, then why has the Christian Church clung to the tradition of celibacy? What messages are being given by a practice which appears to exclude rather than include other people in the way we come to God? How are we to be celibate nowadays? My intention in each of these last three chapters is to examine what it means to be a chaste, poor, obedient person in today's world and Church. The tradition has lessons for our understanding but in these final pages I am telescoping its lessons and concentrating in particular on the ways in which the religious orders have moved forward or been helped forward over the last two decades. This is a time when dialogue between the Church and the world and between the religious and lay life have been most beneficial to the Church.

There were intimations of what this dialogue might mean in a number of things the Roman Catholic Church's second Vatican Council did to change the way we think and, above all, in its exhortation that we be alive to the signs of the times. The question of the vows is a case in point. For a start the Council laicized the content of the vows; it said that a degree of chastity, poverty and obedience is incumbent on every Christian. What makes the religious different is that they *commit* themselves to following Jesus in this way; they make this commitment the matter of a formal promise and ask the Church to identify them in terms of their promise. It is this promising which is at the heart of religious profession, rather than the practice of following a chaste,

poor, obedient Jesus. For all Christians follow the same Jesus and
hear the same vocation or call to love.

When I was a young nun, the vows were named as poverty,
chastity and obedience, in that order. As one wag at the Tite
Street novices' course put it, 'Poverty was not having it, chastity
was not doing it and obedience was not wanting it'. The vows
were things which one took, and which were supposed to have
their own momentum. The second Vatican Council changed the
order, and put chastity first; it also changed the emphasis. Over
the past twenty years there have been enormous shifts in the way
in which religious perceive themselves. The vows are seen less as
things and more as *ways of being*. They commit us to conversion
rather than promising instant change. For this reason there has
been a movement away from renunciation towards acceptance
and affirmation; there has been a reaction to all that was repressive
in former practice and a corresponding growth both in freedom
and in responsibility. The watershed of *Humanae Vitae* has had
its parallels for religious and, significantly, these touch the same
area of human experience, where we are trying to come to God as
human, embodied people. For this reason we are faced with quite
new questions nowadays and with far fewer answers. The answers
which worked in the past belong to questions we are no longer
asking. In their own time they had enormous importance and an
inner validity based in the fact that they belonged to a
homogeneous culture, that of a distinctive group within the
Churches, the religious. In our own times the edges are more
blurred; it is much less clear who and what belongs and who and
what does not. Above all the conversation the Church has asked
us to have with the world is leading us to places and ideas we have
not thought to visit. For this reason I cannot rehearse the old
arguments in these three final chapters; I cannot be quite certain
which are the appropriate and which the inappropriate questions.
All I know is that the contexts in which it is important to raise
them are emerging more clearly all the time.

Recent history

For the previous four hundred years, more and more orders had
proliferated to answer the needs experienced by an increasing
number of disadvantaged groups in society. There had been
brothers to give religious education, sisters to care for orphans

and unmarried mothers, whole groups dedicated to the care of the dying or of the poor and underprivileged, missionaries to take the good news to the New World, India or Africa. Development was lateral rather than progressive; it was tied up with increasing social development. Because education gives social mobility the religious life made an attractive option for generous, well-meaning, intelligent women and men. It was Florence Nightingale who wrote (to the newly converted Henry Manning):

> You do not know what a home the Catholic Church is. And what is she to you compared with what she would be to me? No one can tell, no man can tell, what she is to women, their training, their discipline, their hopes, their home . . . For what training is there compared to that of the Catholic nun? I have seen something of different kinds of nun, am no longer young and do not speak from enthusiasm but from experience. There is nothing like the training (in these days) which the Sacred Heart or the Order of St Vincent gives to women. (Quoted in the *Dublin Review*, 1915)

Florence Nightingale wrote from experience, as one professional woman judging the formation or training of other professional women, and was impressed by the opportunities afforded to women in the religious life. They lived within a context which both allowed and encouraged them to develop. The efforts of Mary Ward and the other early pioneers had not been in vain. When she looked at the nuns she knew, Florence Nightingale perceived too that they were held and contained in such a way that they could develop within specific relationships, namely those they enjoyed with each other. Their communities constituted ready-made domestic space.

Creating carrier space

Within the tradition of the monastic religious life this domestic space had actually dictated the physical layout of convents and monasteries during the medieval period. I quote from a paper by Roberta Gilchrist on the archaeology of medieval English nunneries.

A sample of eight nunnery plans and eight monastery plans of comparable size and date were considered. The results of the analyses suggest that:

1. The nunneries had a higher relative asymmetry from their carrier space than the monasteries, i.e., it was more difficult to gain access to the nuns' cloister from their surrounding precincts.

2. The average number of stages of permeability from the carrier space (levels of access from the precinct) was higher for nunneries.

3. The most segregated component of the complex differed in female and male houses. In the nunneries the dorter, the communal sleeping area of the nuns, was most secluded. In the monasteries, the chapter house, the heart of the community where daily business was transacted, was the most inaccessible to the external secular world.

4. The relative asymmetry of the sacristy (the male liturgical space) in nunneries was the most accessible point, so that the priest could avoid entering the female cloister. In monasteries, sacristies were part of the deepest space, with the function of storing sacred vessels reflected by the lack of permeability.

I find this idea intriguing; the carrier space, in archaeological terms, was the shell of the building which protected it from the 'external secular world' or environment in which the nunnery or monastery was set. Archaeological spatial analysis enables us to see the cloister 'in terms of boundaries' and to observe how those who lived within it defended their deepest, most sacred space not from each other but from those who did not share their values. This they did by constructing walls to make a statement in bricks and mortar about what it was that they held most dear; they embodied the boundaries of their personal space. Accessibility or permeability was restricted, even for those men who served the nunneries by providing the Mass. The nuns, it seems, frequently built their cloisters to the north of their church and, in so far as the church building is an architectural icon representing the cross, this put the women religious at the right side of the dying Christ, in the place occupied by Mary, his mother, in medieval Christian art. 'Religious architecture is dominated by symbolic content and not functional form.' The men put their cloisters to the south at the left side of the church, or of the dying Jesus, as though his suffering gave them permission to go to a place of weakness where the beloved disciple is to be found; the women meanwhile were led into claiming their strength by identifying with the first Christ-bearing woman.

What kind of statements have religious men and women been making since the second Vatican Council; what have we been doing with our domestic space? On one level this question is about how we have been using our convents and monasteries — for architecture enables us to make symbolic statements in stone — but above all it is addressed to how we have been living inside our own bodies. What symbolic statements are being made when people abandon the anonymity of religious dress or religious names and have to face the world without recognizable protection? What symbolic questions are we forced to look at when we find we have money to spend on ourselves and upon our appearance? What issues lie behind these questions? I see them as being addressed very specifically to the body and to the way in which all of us — religious and lay Christians — accept that we are embodied people. This is no longer an area of experience, mine or the world's, which I can dodge in the name of vowed celibacy; if anything the vow asks me to look at the question far more seriously than I ever needed to do in the past. So I have to reflect on what is being said nowadays about celibacy: how is it to be lived by religious and lay people alike in a world which swings uneasily between liberalism and repression, and where sexuality and sexual practice are alternately magicalized and denigrated. I have to ask how I can be embodied in ways that are honest and sane, with real friends, real relationships and a positive attitude towards sexuality.

Personal space which excludes other people is the domestic space of someone very wounded or betrayed. For most of us it is space we share with the people who carry and contain us, the people we carry and contain. The vows of those who profess chastity ask us how we use this space, how we fill it and live within it; the vows of those who are committed to have and to hold each other raise the same questions.

Sexuality and sensuality

In conversation with my married and single friends, women and men, I am learning to de-magicalize some of my ideas about sex. I

73

am beginning to understand that we are all on the same journey and that it is a journey into accepting our own sensuality, our own place in the animal kingdom and material world. We are called to live within our bodies and not apart from them. The route taken by people who live within a named one-to-one relationship is to do this journeying in the company of another person and, in time, with any children of their union. The route taken by single people is to do this journeying alone or in the company of named friends who share what one of my single friends has called her 'heart-space'. Religious women or men do this journeying in the company of their communities and, with changing age-structures and new forms of apostolic work and opportunity, are learning that these are manifold. The communities to which I belong are many and various: I was born into some, such as my family and my European context; some I have chosen, such as my religious community; and some have been given to me, such as my colleagues at work, friends and those who love me. With each of these — and their edges are blurred — I am invited to make the journey into integrity, the journey away from an excessively 'spiritualized' view of what it is to be a person with a body and a real live context.

There are common features to this journeying. In the past we have perhaps been more careful to say what kept us apart rather than what we might learn in common. The witness of the sexually active life was ignored while that of the sexually inactive life became attached to ever more unrealistic goals. If the goal of both is owning our earthliness, then what do people who try to reach it with sex have to say to those who try to reach it without? I use the words 'sexually inactive' cautiously. On one level our language has not yet really caught up with our practice. Many religious resent this expression; they feel it has been hard enough to own that they are sexual beings, and that the carpet is once again being whipped away from under their feet. Our God is a God of desire, the God of *eros*, as well as the God who is moved by human need, the God of *agapē*. In the name of this desiring God I continue to use the words 'sexually active' and 'sexually inactive' because I see sensuality as the common denominator, our bodies being the place where we experience desire. Once some kind of conversation has begun to gain momentum, then the relationship of the religious life to lay life can be addressed the

74

other way round, and the lessons of the celibate life be spelt out again and more clearly.

My sexually-active friends remind me that love-making is about entering into domestic space as a lover and not as a warrior. Love-making is a context for holding. One of my oldest friends sent me the draft of a chapter entitled, 'Christian eroticism'. I read it with my eyes popping out of my head, for the language of abandonment she used took me to places I had presumed lie close to the altar and the cross. The word 'passion' carries the double meaning of pain and pleasure and it is not by chance that the language of mysticism has relied so heavily on bridal imagery. To come this close to another person is to make oneself vulnerable and open and to reveal the depths of one's desire. My married friends take a far greater risk than I do; they risk letting another human being this close, while I back off in the name of God. They tantalize me in other ways too, by forcing me to realize that I actually have quite a good deal. If ever I sleep badly it is not because I have been woken by someone else thrashing around beside me, or a husband falling heavily into bed after a working dinner . . . I have had broken nights because I have looked after other people's children at night. At its worst this meant being woken by a white-faced little creature who said, 'Please sister, I've been sick and I've lost my false tooth down the loo and mummy will be furious.' I remember having mixed feelings as I went fishing for the offending tooth. But these are isolated events and not part of a pattern of broken nights and exhausting days.

What I learn from my sexually-active friends is that sex asserts the importance of the body in enabling us to be at home within the carrier space of our relationships and loves. It is paradigmatic; how people make love reflects how they are in the outer world. For stealth and hypocrisy, abuse and sexism are unmasked where they cannot hide behind fine words. Tenderness, mutuality and humour find their natural language in the gestures of love and of passion. The warrior is competitive, out to prove something, where the lover woos, cherishes and holds. This is expressed most closely in love-making but is true at the breakfast table too, or when the bank statement comes in.

What I believe professed religious can learn from this is that we are too easily able to hide from the demands of intimacy. We ask married people to carry the burden of that part of the Christian story for us and we berate them when they fail. The strength of reaction we feel when marriages break down must be some kind of comment about the investment we are making in marriage. We need it to work because we know intimacy to be important; we need it to work because married people are carrying some of our scripts for us. It is quite useful to notice that this is what is going on. Then the burden of idealization can be removed from married people and professed religious alike. Our mistake is to have imagined that celibacy is about suppressing the place of intimacy in our own lives. Yet why should religious escape the common call to relate to other people with tenderness, mutuality and humour? Why should we be exempt from the challenge to go against the weakness of stealth and hypocrisy, the abuse of sexism and exploitation? Why should we live blandly and without passion? My married friends and I say the same version of the Lord's prayer; we both pray 'Thy kingdom come'; it seems to me that the common Christian task is to live out of the values of this kingdom and not duck them in the name of a promise or vow. Jesus berated the religious leaders who gave their money under pledge to the Temple as 'corban' and failed to honour the fourth commandment. Where we make the gift of ourselves by vows of chastity are we buying into or out of the call to love?

These are the questions I hear when I listen to the experience of those who are sexually active among my friends. But I have questions to put to them as well. If I have a tendency to magicalize sex I believe that they have a tendency to magicalize chastity. If I have a tendency to try to live outside my body and not to hear it when it tells me to rest and to look after myself and to take care to adorn myself as the beloved of God, then they have a tendency not to look further than the end of their noses, to forget that their domestic space — their home or family — is a place for reaching out to other people, to embrace those who are the fruit of bodies other than their own. Where we both acknowledge our sensuality we can talk to each other about what it means to grow to God as bodily people and see what a rough deal the tradition has given to the flesh.

The body as image of the flesh and the world

Many of the unspoken scripts which underlie what I have just been saying appear to relate more to the experience of women than men. Of course there are men who have been woken in the night, of course there are men who find it all too hard to grasp their manhood, either as warrior or as lover. They too have fallen victim to the same hierarchical thinking which poisons relationships by setting up tensions between women and men, body and soul, earth and heaven. These scripts are worth uncovering, however, because the body and women's bodies in particular have been made to carry messages which demonstrate how hard we find it to be physical people in a material world. We reach for the stars, forgetting that they too are made of dust as we are. We crave for release instead of desiring to experience our dependence on the earth, our need to have our feet firmly on the ground. We forget that the God who made us crowned creation with our making and did not give us being apart from creation but as part of it. God found our creatureliness good, and God's Word became flesh.

God the embodier gave us the whole world to become carrier space; it is we who fragment our experience and divide it into what belongs to the day and what to the night. We name some of our experience with pride — usually that which belongs to the mind and its achievements, or the 'soul' and its finer flights. Some we name with alarm and shame. Whereas our bodies are the place where we are invited to be what we are, body people. If the profession of religious celibacy is about anything it has to be about standing in this place and being resolved to remain there, refusing to side with the myths that denigrate either women or the body they are supposed to typify or the earth out of which we are all made.

Celibates are needed at this place because it is here that the connections are made and we see that there is a definite link between what we say about bodies in one area of our experience and how we treat the bodily and incarnated wherever we meet it. We have no axe to grind and, at the same time, we have every axe to grind and the energy to do this grinding, because vowed celibacy is about promising not to be possessive in our relationships, whether with other people, the ones who share our carrier space, or with the wider world and with the earth. I used to use the word non-possessive rather blithely until I began to learn of my desire to possess and be possessed. It tripped off my tongue far too easily and was usually coupled with the other cliché about being non-manipulative. I think what I am trying to say is that I believe we are all asked to move beyond a rhetoric which sets up the oppressors against the oppressed, the oppressed against the oppressors. Our bodies are the place where we are invited to demonstrate that this is happening. In this way God's word becomes flesh in today's world, today's values and within today's carrier space.

The tradition has sometimes fallen down on this message or given us partial glimpses of what we are supposed to be doing. More recently there has been a tendency to go the other way, to experiment and question the extent to which anyone can do without sex. As a result of the work I do as a spiritual director and in giving retreats to religious I am aware that the religious life has lost some of its virgins, but it has gained people who are resolved to live with their eyes open and who have lost some of their ignorance along with their innocence. Where there is balance and harmony, when we admit that growth as an embodied person will mean making mistakes, both professed religious and lay people need each other to be reminded that the real journey is towards mutuality and love, towards identifying with that of which we are made, and finding the Creator within all that makes us creature. This journey takes time; in this chapter I have done no more than indicate where the journey leads and explore some of the questions this raises. A time will come when it will be possible to furnish answers and address more directly the connection that John Donne put before us when he wrote: 'From thinking us all soul, neglecting thus our mutual duties, Lord deliver us'.

9

A context for owning:
poverty

As creatures we are broken people whose lives can feel desperately fragmented. And Christianity is matched to human need. Of its essence, it is a religion for broken people, for people who can acknowledge their need of salvation. Over the past twenty years the 'universal call to holiness' offered so enticingly to all Christians by the second Vatican Council has led us in turn forward and sideways. Often it has led us away from the lessons God would have us learn in inviting us to accept our personal and corporate truth. Instead of calling upon God from the depths of our need for redemption, we have been side-tracked into presenting a shiny-bright version of ourselves to God, the Church and the world. The call to holiness offered to all has led us to claim holiness too quickly; we are in danger of losing our sense of sin and our sense of God's saving redeeming love. Once upon a time our projections were at least contained within the body of believers: the saints were saints, we were sinners; the religious life was for those who aspired to perfection, lay life was for the rest. Now we risk being unable to do this containing; a tidied-up Church looks with distaste at an untidy world. Where has compassion gone? When the place of sin is denied within our Christian rhetoric, we soon 'ose the ability to name our personal hurt and pain and ambiguity; we begin to grow cold. How can we look poverty in the face and take possession of the real treasure of our human and personal identity? We are lovable because we are God's, not because we are rich or good, nor because we are holy.

In the vocabulary of contemporary spirituality we talk very easily about wholeness and integration; we have more trouble with sin and pain. At heart we seem set to redeem ourselves. Perfectionism has always had a tendency to rear her ugly head and nowadays she woos us ingratiatingly with fresh wares. Today's onwardly mobile Christian is as much at risk from the desire to be pleasing to God as ever our unenlightened pre-conciliar forebears were. If anything the mechanics of our cult make this lure more enticing than ever. The monster no longer lives in convents; she is out there in the world doing it in ordinary homes and workplaces with a whole new battery of charms.

And so spirituality and psychology have lain down together like the lion and the lamb and promised us the healing of total integration. With each vogue in turn, from Myers Briggs workshops through endless magical mystical byways to the Enneagram, we have danced, prayed, sung and massaged our way to wholeness. We have given up meat and taken up yoga; we have cut down on eggs and butter and learnt to like skimmed yoghurt and decaffeinated coffee; we have prayed on little stools to the refrain of Taizé chants; we have burnt joss sticks and candles. We have joined the justice and peace group and been on retreat; we have thrown away our rosaries and allowed our confessionals to fall into disrepair. And yet we remain the same riff-raff, the same bunch of oddballs we ever were. There is no harm in this. The only harm is that we might pretend we are not.

What happens to what frightens us?

It could be that we have missed the ways in which the Church's dialogue with the world has given a particular tone and resonance to the conversation we all need to have within ourselves. This is a dialogue about which the tradition was perhaps more honest than we are now. We have been too quick to say we are rich, whereas the tradition enabled us to say that we are poor and not to be frightened by this. When I was little, the greatest term of abuse I could use was to call the other children I played with on the beach at my grandmother's house in France 'crétins'. This was wrong, the adult world explained, because the word was a bastardized form of the honourable word 'Christian'. We were not reproached for cracking jokes that denigrated handicapped people or foreigners. Racist language was part of our everyday culture and stared out at us each morning from the marmalade jar with its golliwog label. We played at climbing Everest and put on our best clothes to watch the Queen's Coronation on television, but equally we went on fighting the war armed with decaying Mickey Mouse gasmasks; our enemies had names, they were Germans and Japanese and we hated them. We chanted the refrain 'Linger longer, Queen of Tonga', but the newspapers stirred us with racist feelings as well by warning us of the dangers of unrestricted immigration. As a Roman Catholic in the heart of non-conformist Birmingham I had no idea of the irony concealed in attempts to make me throw the first stone. My face is white but I am the grandchild of immigrants. Every afternoon I was taken for a walk to the Botanical Gardens. There we would press our noses against the monkey pens and laugh at them for being so stupid; not for being playful or cold and wet or full of fleas, but for being the stupid ones who had got caught. There were other oddities too — like 'non-Catholics'. I had to wait until I was well into my thirties before I first began to question the version of history on which I had been raised; one which presented them as 'the people who took away "our" churches' and lost the true faith. In spite of all Newman's fine intentions, the Birmingham Oratory was making a statement in stone that confirmed every prejudice lurking inside my little ultramontane mind.

Only the liturgy gave me pause, and this is a theme to which I will return. For the Roman Catholic liturgy and sacramental practice and the domestic piety of my youth gave me a context in which to say I was personally a sinner. The baptismal font was huge; I could imagine myself sheltered in it and immersed in water that really would get rid of original sin. The hymn I most enjoyed was 'Lord, for tomorrow and its needs' with its lines about pride and 'mortifying the flesh'. It kept me on tenterhooks. I hovered on the brink of the 'stain of sin' and only just scrambled to safety thanks to Our Lady, my guardian angel and going to confession. I could get into the mood for going to confession by thumping my skinny little chest at the *Agnus Dei* and feeling wonderfully solemn during Advent and Lent. At its worst liturgical practice fed my sense of guilt; at its best it exhilarated me and taught me that I was amazingly complicated and that God knew me and cared about me. It threw up shadows and light in my soul and kept me in touch with my own poverty. I lived in a whirl of projections but somehow the Church enabled me to go on naming the sin within the community of believers and within myself. It allowed me to feel bad, to know myself as a fragmented person. Mistakenly it also made me feel guilty.

I was perfect raw material for the trends of the sixties and seventies. I hungered to hear that wholeness and holiness belonged together; I needed to have my body redeemed by liberalism, my mind expurgated by the faith/justice link, and my conscience transformed by concern for the handicapped, the deprived and the dying. The eighties have continued to feed me with good things; I am losing some of my convictions, however, and regaining my sense of ambiguity. The dialogue which the world has set up in the Churches is a dialogue about the place of minorities. Hence the importance of conducting this conversation in an area where an important role reversal is taking place, where lay people are filling a hole in the Church's life which the religious used to occupy. How do we cope with the altered power structure which this dynamic throws up? What do we do with what frightens us?

Talking about sin

Over the past twenty years, in the attempt to undo the connections that led us to couple sin and guilt (as opposed to sin and the knowledge that God is a saving God), we have stopped talking about sin. We have begun to invalidate our own experience. Nowadays I believe the balance is being redressed. For the reality is that this rhetoric cannot bear the strain of the facts and our conversation with the world is leading us to new insights. A world that contains the arms race, apartheid and Chernobyl, child-abusers, ayatollahs, fallen evangelist superstars and gazumping yuppies challenges our wishy-washy liberalism. Equally a world that is beginning to imitate the Churches by pursuing deviants with all the enthusiasm of an inquisition is a world that demands that we be very clear about what we mean by sin and by the ambiguity of human poverty.

For the past couple of decades Christians, whether lay, ordained or religious, have adopted a caring role in society. With complete conviction we have named poverty as a root evil and worked hard to fight it at national and international level. Why then must the Church always have people who profess vows of poverty? Why does the second Vatican Council recommend poverty to lay people and religious alike? I believe the answer has something to do with the fact that we need a real live context within which we can speak of our deepest need, which is for a saving God. This is not to set up religion as the opponent of the material order, to say that the 'spirit' cannot abide the flesh. If anything we have to be rigorous in defending the God of hi-tech. The point is that in a Church which enables some people to witness to the value of poverty by vowed commitment it is easier for all of us to continue to acknowledge our own. Human fallibility, our personal need of care, our own inherent sinfulness, our fear of death are nudged out when we are not allowed to be imperfect or less than holy; they no longer belong. Hence I believe the helpful stirrings by which we are being asked to listen again to what the Spirit is saying to and in the Churches. Ordinary Christians are reclaiming what was best in the tradition, and orthodoxy is taking up the cause of sin. The 'happy fault' is back in our midst. Over the last year I have heard people asking to reflect on the place of sin in a way that was inconceivable even five years ago.

I believe the real enemy is about to be revealed. Religious perfection is being uncovered for the tyrant she is. She is the Leviathan who swims through our own personal seas and flicks us into power games with a mere swish of her tail. And suddenly we are unmasking her, we are demanding that she stop playing games and start being honest. People who erect the shelter of a neat and tidy front are tempted to find anything untidy intolerable, particularly when it lurks inside themselves. People who have a problem accepting their own anxiety or dismay can take heart. The gospels are good news for obsessives as much as for the rest of us who are merely neurotics.

For the Jesus whom I meet in the pages of the gospels is bent on undermining our assumptions about good and evil. He enables us to recognize the dark. He brings us up short when we try to become perfect and exposes the mechanics of projection. His stories speak of the presence of the dark and the light within; they are about pairs of brothers — the nameless rich man and Lazarus who lies bleeding at his gate, the elder son and the prodigal, the Pharisee and the publican. His own story likewise was lived out in the presence of ambiguity; Martha and Mary, Peter and Judas. He died somewhere crucial, in the place where all Christians receive their identity, between a believing and a blaspheming thief.

Naming the dark within

Earlier this year I had a revelation on a London bus. The number 12 takes an hour to go from Oxford Circus to the outer darkness of Forest Hill. I caught it on Regent Street and scrambled up to the last remaining seat on the top deck, at the back on the right hand side. After a while I heard a voice calling out, 'Madam, madam'. I turned round and saw behind me on the left a woman in her twenties. Her face was puffy and bruised; her bottom teeth had been knocked out; she was drinking from a can of beer and was asking me for a light. She had left hers on her pitch, she explained and so, incongruously, I imagined she had been to a football match. I looked at her with total recognition, with a degree of identification that would have astonished our fellow travellers. I saw all my own pain and hurt in her face and in her battered mouth; I heard the polite institutionalized voice saying, 'Madam, madam', knowing all the right words, the mechanics of survival; I saw the outward signs of personal weakness and need, the beer can and soggy cigarette. Inside myself I wept. I wonder what she saw when she looked at me? I wonder if I will ever understand the extent to which I need to learn the lessons of darkness that she imaged for me as she asked me for a light.

The story has a follow-up. In a sense it had to because it was so shockingly apposite and well-timed; my shadow appeared to me with human features at a moment when I could recognize her and look on her with love. I needed her and need her still. The following day when cycling down Bond Street I took a slightly different route from my usual one and found myself drawing up at some red traffic lights in Mayfair. Then I heard her voice, rasping out the words, 'News, evening news'. She was selling newspapers from her 'pitch'. The odds against our meeting again, our meeting the next day, within half a mile of where I work, must have been extraordinarily high. She can come to me for light and I can go to her news, for information. And so we can find that each of us lies bleeding at the other's gate.

Naming pain and hurt and ambiguity like this is easier when there is a picture or an event to attach it to. This is why the rich man went to hell. He failed to recognize the place of poverty within his own story. He could not own the parts of him that lay bleeding within because he ignored them at his gate. He did not

84

know he needed saving. His culture and value system had taught him to despise failure and to be rigorous in pursuing success. His religion backed him up by giving him theological hooks on which to hang his assumptions. Only in the afterlife did the reversals take place and from Abraham's bosom Lazarus was powerless to help in a way he had never been on earth. For the poor are powerful and it is a myth to pretend that they are not. There is immense energy in claiming the power of our own personal poverty, in owning our weakness and our pain. It is the energy of conversion.

Naming the world's dark

This is true at the level of our own inner experience and at the level of our domestic experience but also at international level. I am reminded of this by a remarkable passage from the novel of a Canadian author, Jo Anne Williams Bennett, *Downfall People*. Her north American hero, Likki, faces Ibn Sinna, her native lover.

> Likki was uncomfortably aware that she had wanted him to say he believed in witchcraft. And not just Ibn Sinna. She wanted all of Africa to believe in it, to remain in a cradle of savage belief, a state of primitive purity, as a kind of monument to the white man's nostalgia and regret — a place where he might wander for an interlude of archetypal quiet when the chaos of his own busy centuries grew intolerable. She wanted Africa to be a kind of psychic tourist resort; to be taken, pressed firmly into the past, and held there, because in her own time and place she could not be master. These ideas, of course, were not peculiar to Likki but were general throughout her culture; the price of them now was paid by, among others, the under-nourished children of Segou, who died needlessly of a preventable disease in a squalid, waterless village because Africa had been equated with the unconscious past and what happened there was not real.

In this passage the dynamics of projection are exposed and revealed as the cultural heritage of the rich: 'in her own time and place she could not be master'; our inadequacy, our vain attempts at wholeness are doomed to make us ignore what really needs attention. And the people who die are the little ones, the 'undernourished children' of our unfulfilled dreams.

There are whole nations that lie bleeding at our gate. They carry the 'treasures of darkness' (Isaiah 45.3), and they call us to conversion or change. Our collective human and ecclesial experience is of fragmentation and it is within this mess, not apart from it, that we are asked to be holy. In the name of religious perfection we too easily attempt to short circuit the process by sentimentalizing poverty, by idolizing the 'primitive purity' of whole peoples who live more simply than we do in the first world, by appearing to crave for low-tech 'archetypal quiet' because we exaggerate the strain of hi-tech living. In the name of religious perfection we set ourselves up as the healers and the carers, the ones who can crack the problem, unconsciously adopting a superior tone and position in our dealings with the weak. I have always been haunted by the story of Damian the leper, the priest who dropped his bowl of shaving water onto his feet one morning and felt nothing and went out into his leper village able to say 'we' for the first time. In the name of religious perfection we fail to see the blindingly clear message that there is a middle ground, a place where the strong and the weak can talk to each other and that it lies within each one of us. In this place, which is holy ground, we learn the importance of dialogue, of talking to each other about our needs, of sharing our common treasures — whether they be those we have learnt in the day or in the night. In this place we learn to lose our fears of each other, our projections are quite disarmed. The fragmentation remains but we are no longer bleeding from neglect, we pour oil in each other's wounds and bind each other up. The gate is no longer a barrier or a hurdle; it has become the place where we are open with each other and welcome each other in, the place of mutuality.

Bringing the darkness into the light

I have suggested that within the Christian Churches we have a ready-made context for attempting to effect this resolution or conversion, a ready-made gate. Liturgy — the words and music and silence in which we dramatize our condition before God — must name human brokenness. The creeping sickness which is beginning to afflict our collects and prefaces — where even Lent is now called 'this season of joy' and despair no longer has a voice — must be unmasked. Every liturgical celebration has a teaching function; it sets up ideas and reactions in us by informing our thinking and our feeling. But what theology informs our practice? Who is the God we come to worship in church? A God who cannot bear the sight of sin and who despises human pain? A God who is terrified of weakness and whom we should not risk approaching with our own? A heavy God who reads the political weeklies and only likes ideologically-sound prayers of intercession? Or a God who delights in us as we are; the God of compassion who allows us to stumble and grope our way forwards, asking questions and owning our doubt, uneasily seeking the union of all our personal and collective broken bits by allowing them to talk to each other and listening to the wisdom they bring together into the light. Only in the name of this God can we safely make vows of poverty and seek to minister within a broken Church and a broken world.

Ministering to human need

For this reason too we need women ministers — ordained and unordained. This is not my main thesis in writing this chapter, but I find that it makes a significant afterword. Women can help because the cultural scripts we carry have constantly put us in a place of weakness. We know our way round this place and, while it is painful for us, it is not somewhere we fear. Biblical and theological scripts have put us, with Eve, in the place of sin. In the new language women are learning in today's Church we have discovered that we are not guilty of this sin. Our mistake has been to believe the messages that made us feel guilty. In this we misnamed our sin. The irony is that we are ideally placed to help everyone learn that we need be afraid neither of weakness nor of sin, only of our vain attempts to avoid either. Women are throwing off the mantle of guilt and learning the song of freedom. In this song words like sin, failure and weakness can be used without fear, and so the words joy, love and forgiveness be rediscovered with fresh force: 'My soul rejoices in God who is my Saviour' (Luke 1.47). Mary's *Magnificat* is being used by liberation theology as a paeon of freedom. At heart, however, it remains the song of a poor woman who knew her need of God. As poor people we can sing it as we choose, as women or as men.

10

A context for choosing: obedience

'I think that must be the hardest one, well certainly the one I'd find hardest.' The vow of obedience has a bad reputation; in the popular mind, it dehumanizes, it makes tyrants out of some and destroys the free will of others. Power corrupts and religious power is the most dangerous of all, for it appears to be backed up by divine sanction, and this has sometimes been read as a human ticket to megalomania. At the Tite Street novices' course I did a role play exercise of three different conversations between religious superiors and their 'subjects'. Each of these was supposed to depict unhelpful or helpful ways in which we learn to become discerning or obedient people because it is important to model good and bad understandings of authority to anyone contemplating taking such a vow.

The first was between a novice and her novice director. The novice had just returned from three weeks working in a hospice. During her time there she had had some really important insights into the difference between loneliness and solitude and wanted to talk these through with the woman who was responsible for her formation as a religious sister. The novice mistress meanwhile had her own agenda; she had been brought up to avoid anything painful and found it threatening to be asked to do so. To cope with her anxiety she belittled the novice's experience by checking out whether she had had enough to eat, whether she had slept well and whether she had been careful to make friends in her host community. Behind the pastiche a very serious question was being raised; how does any novice effect the change from one set of values to another while maintaining her freedom and integrity? The first set of values had provided her with a useful way of organizing her life before she entered the convent. There she had learnt that loneliness was to be avoided and here she was experiencing it for the first time in her life. Moreover the experience was not the bad one she feared. So much so that she was seeking her way towards a new vocabulary to try to describe what was happening to her. The novice director, by being so crass and concentrating on externals, failed to pick up an important cue in the young woman's attempt to feed from the wisdom of the order's self-understanding. As the younger woman sought to learn from her and so to converse with the order's collective wisdom, the novice mistress failed to meet her where she was. In this way the novice's wholly appropriate attempts to become dependent upon the order, to lean upon it to learn its wisdom, were met by a refusal.

In the second conversation a professed sister in her late fifties resolutely sat on the edge of her chair saying to her local community superior that 'everything was all right', that nothing was the matter and that she just needed to be told what to do as then her problems would go away. Her principal anxiety, it emerged, was that she felt she could not pray. The superior in question, who had read all the right books, attended all the right workshops and kept up to date with the Church's thinking, remained resolutely uncommitted to a contemporary understanding of obedience. She oscillated, at one moment adopting a caring, listening attitude, at the next provoking and bullying. When pushed into a corner by the pain of a sister who could only repeat that everything was fine, she resorted to clichés: 'Jesus calls us to carry the cross, you have a problem, you cannot expect an easy ride.' In this way she totally failed to come near the sister's real anxiety. In fact the sister was in a blind panic; she was approaching retirement age; she had no idea what the future held for her, all her self-understanding had been mediated to her through her working life as a very able hospital matron; ahead of her she saw nothing but meaninglessness and she could not face a meaningless God in prayer. In the face of this blank future she resorted to the infantile tactic of saying 'Tell me what to do', 'You say "jump", I say "how high?" ' Both of them colluded in inhibiting any real conversation; both emerged with their worst fears about the value of discernment firmly in place. They were pushed into independence, a place where neither could offer the other any kind of support — the loneliness the novice in the first role play had been right to fear — and they could not grow away from this.

The third conversation had a shorter brief. The rubric my colleague and I had prepared simply read, 'A junior professed religious is discussing his/her first job with the provincial superior of his/her congregation. The provincial has been asked by the headteacher of one of the order's schools to make a science graduate available to them. The young religious in question has just spent three months working in a retreat centre with young people . . .' I took the part of the provincial and, as this was supposed to be an interview which demonstrated the positive side of discernment and its place in understanding how we can safely make vows of obedience, I had to listen hard.

As the conversation got under way I checked out the enthusiasm with which the religious spoke of her experience in the retreat house. On my desk I had a favourable report on the time she had spent there; it had certain reservations — was she a good team member or were some of her schemes too madcap and wild? I asked her about her experience of the team meetings. I asked her what it was in her own life and faith journey that led her to believe she might have something valuable to share with the young people in question. I heard her speak with more than enthusiasm, with a clear-headed conviction about what it meant to her to do youth work. Again I had an external point of reference in my own mind; I am aware of the 'one-step' theory which demonstrates that in youth work, as in many other areas of pastoral work, the person who is best able to do the guiding is the person who is one step ahead — as opposed to a long way ahead — of those being guided. If this is objectively the case, however, I still needed more positive and subjective clarification. I asked her to tell me more about how she had worked, and began to see where the word 'madcap' might have come from. Her method had been to use a lot of paint and dance and clay for modelling, and also movement. In a team which relied rather heavily on the verbal, this would not necessarily meet with a great deal of understanding.

As we talked I found it important to put my dilemma to her. The headteacher at St Mark's needed a science graduate and she was one. Her answer impressed me. She spoke with conviction and honesty describing the strong negative feelings she had for this idea. She was afraid her knowledge of chemistry was rusty and was frightened of laboratory work with teenagers. I could not put her down with remarks about carrying the cross or being prepared to go against her own will for a greater good. The greater good might be to face her fear of failure. The greater good might be to put her into a context in which she could exercise her gifts for youth work. A retreat house would be an obvious one, but before our very eyes another was being suggested to us. I found myself asking her what she would feel if we were to explore together the idea of her being sent in to do chaplaincy work in St Mark's. My task would be to sound out the headteacher, hers I suggested would be to find out if other schools in that area already had chaplaincies, that is to say what support she could find in the local set-up, what facilities they might share in common, what youth hostels or residential centres there were in the area which might be useful to them for retreat weekends, etc. Equally she undertook to look around and see what chemistry refresher courses might be available.

We both completed the interview feeling that we were open to creative and God-directed possibilities, that we had both been listened to and heard and that we were both committed to investigating the future further. Moreover I had the satisfaction of having a hunch that I was honouring the request of the head-teacher in ways which took his request further than he had envisaged. When she arrived at his school this young woman would come with a real sense of purpose, whatever the work she would in fact be doing there.

Images of religious obedience

Behind each of these three conversations lay a different understanding of religious obedience. Each is worth uncovering but I am finding increasingly that this uncovering is best done when it asks what model of human development it conceals. In this way the questions the Church and world put to the religious life have some kind of focus. In the first I have suggested that the novice was asking for some help in interpreting her experience. Her understanding was that she had the right to expect this work of interpretation to be done within the framework of the order's own self-understanding. On this level she was asking to become dependent. I find this a perfectly legitimate request; she could not interpret her experience freely until she had had a chance to be exposed to the collective wisdom of the order. In the second the sister in question was at an interim stage; she was so scared by her sad, anxious feelings that she had moved to somewhere negative where she was blocking all the superior's attempts to move into a genuine conversation with her. The superior too was somewhere rather similar. She was working out of an isolationist model of religious obedience where orders do indeed come from on high and are to be received as the divine wisdom. In the third example, on the other hand, a different model was emerging, one of interdependence. Both the provincial superior and the sister in question were searching for God's will together. They were in the Zen garden I described in chapter six, seeking God's will in a named context and open to whatever it might be. They were dependent on each other's openness and good will and on the goodness of a God who is attempting to come near to our projects and concerns, not to hide from them.

This is the God who gives us our feelings as a context for choosing, a God who works with the known in order to help us to move to the unknown. We are right to be suspicious of vowed obedience where it does no more than confirm our worst fears that to promise to obey someone is to hand over any sense of responsibility, either for engaging with the decisions by which we come to make Christian choices or for carrying these through and being accountable for what we do.

Discernment, mission and accountability

The three role play exercises I have described illustrate aspects of what is meant by discernment. Together in conversation and in prayer we seek to know what God wills for us by listening both to the movement of the Spirit within ourselves and to the movement of this same Spirit in the desires and needs of the wider Church. God speaks to us in our feelings and leads us beyond a simple rationalization of what we hear there. We are taught to listen to positive and negative aspects of our own experience and to realize that both have their place. We are taught not to make simple equations. Feeling bad does not mean that we are bad; feeling good does not mean that we are good. The framework in which we are asked to discern or listen to the voice of God within is one where both the negative and the positive have their place. I am not advocating a simplistic appropriation of the Christian story, just one which allows God to work with the grace-filled given of our own gifts and talents and nature. For precisely because our feelings are ordinarily beyond our conscious control, they are the place where God can communicate most persuasively with us.

So what informs our feelings? How seriously do we take them? Do we listen to their messages? Above all, do we talk to anyone about them? The tradition's respect for religious vowed obedience is a measure of the esteem the Church has always had for the authoritative voice both of individual and of collective conscience. Beyond anarchy moreover, the tradition has proposed that there be a safety net to enable individuals to pick up on the feelings of the Church and world — for God is speaking in these too. My private dreams have to be refined by the wider dreams represented by the life, death and resurrection of Jesus. My private dreams — those I hear in the midst of me — have to be informed by the living body of Jesus present in our collective midst. If I am vowed to religious obedience, I am committed to speaking my truth and listening to the truth. I am committed to being aware that there is a difference between the two, and this is as hard for religious superiors as for religious subjects. We cling to certainty because it enables us to plan a chessboard version of life, one in which a bishop is a bishop, a pawn is a pawn. We know how both move and find it disruptive when the one develops gifts we had thought appropriate to the other.

The religious superior who takes the theology of mission seriously is committed to discernment. Any sending of individuals which she or he does is informed by an intimate knowledge of the one who is being sent. Where I really know someone, I love that person in weakness and in strength, whereas strangers may fill me with fear, because I do not know what motivates them. The one who is sent or missioned is someone known to me by name, not an idealized version of her- or himself. In this way I am enabled to be realistic; I avoid being brutal or treating people like corks whose task it is to plug the gaping holes in my institution. The religious subject is likewise committed to discernment, accurate self-knowledge and openness. Such openness enables one to become more indifferent or personally free from private scheming. It enables grace to build on nature, nature on grace.

Obedience has a third moment. The first is discernment, the second is the act of sending or mission and the third is the moment represented by the word 'accountability'. Just as discernment means that I am not going to be asked to do anything which it is genuinely beyond my powers to perform, so accountability keeps in contact with the real me in the real work I am being asked to do. The practice of discernment does not dry up once an individual has begun to work as an apostolic person in a given area of need. Accountability means keeping the lines of communication open, being prepared to talk about what is going well and what is going badly in one's personal work and life. In this way, once again, I am accepting that my feelings are important, that God is communicating to me through them and that vowed obedience commits me to listen to what I am hearing. I am not condemned to do this listening alone; I am given a framework within which I can try to understand what I am hearing from those with whom I work and the world and Church for whom I work.

This joint listening has to be done with extreme sensitivity or else it can be very threatening. I have seen grown men rooted to the spot by fear of this process because it has recently been introduced in a seemingly arbitrary way into the way in which they have traditionally exercised their ministry. I have seen younger people, admirably, radiating the confidence that comes from a good experience of accountability. Practice makes perfect, but over and above that an intelligent understanding of the place of accountability can dispel some of the fearsome myths that surround it. I have friends who work in public corporations or for the civil service who undergo a much more rigorous process of assessment each year than most Church people would let themselves in for. I have friends who have had to pass really difficult examinations in order to obtain the professional status which enables them to listen to other people's confidences in a way in which, if I am honest, I suppose I consider my right. Why should they be accountable and why should I not be so? Why does accountability frighten so many religious people? We all fear failure, certainly. But why?

Behind our reluctance to be obedient people in this sense, there lurks a messiah complex of the grand proportions which so alarm us in the practice of a Simon Stylites. Behind our reluctance to be obedient people lies a fear of the otherness of God. Beyond our reluctance to be obedient people lie years of bad memories, of ways in which the tradition has abused the good will of generous people. Beyond our reluctance to be obedient people lies a reluctance to allow God to reveal a little more of the divine will, progressively, all the time. We want things to remain constant and unchanging so that we can defend our little patch of the vineyard against invasion and against the erosion of time. Yet the God of revelation calls us to constant change and to reinterpret the divine will as we go along. The obedience we are asked to practise within the relationships we name by vow need not frighten us; it exists to protect us from our fears.

In this sense it is a valid context for choosing and one which demands that our choices be Christian choices, that is to say, choices which are consonant with those which Jesus made. It is easy to sound sentimentally sanctimonious in speaking of the choices of Jesus. In point of fact they are the ones which every Christian faces and at their most stark are those set out for us in the Book of Deuteronomy: 'I call heaven and earth to witness against you today: I set before you life or death, blessing or curse. Choose life, then, so that you and your descendants may live, in the love of Yahweh your God, clinging to him' (Deuteronomy 30.19). We are to choose life, freedom, hope. In this we are following the choosing that Jesus did and committing ourselves to an experience based on his. In this sense our journey will take us into and through the experience of death, into and through the experience of slavery and into and through the experience of despair. These are Christian places in that Jesus has been there before us. He has harrowed all our hells. But they are the ambiguous places where Yahweh his God went before him as well: 'Yahweh has chosen to dwell in a thick cloud' (1 Kings 8.13). In the thick cloud God is revealed as mystery and presence but as obscurity and absence as well. In our choosing of life, God will have each of these faces in turn, and Jesus too from the place of despair asked why God had abandoned him. How may we go there safely, as people whose root option is for the gift of life? What does the present-day tradition, the voice of today's Church have to say to this question? How can we confound those who fear that vowed obedience does not lead through the cross to glory?

When things go wrong

In order to explore this question, I find myself turning to an improbable document for information. The Roman Catholic Church's *Code of Canon Law* does not exactly make bedside reading. Within its pages, however, lies a vision of ecclesiology or attempt at self-understanding which I find makes a reasoned and lucid presentation of the insights of the second Vatican Council. One of my favourite texts is contained in another volume, the *Index to the Code of Canon Law*. This makes fascinating if occasionally scary reading. An instance: the word 'maturity' appears once in the index, with references that make it clear that what is being alluded to is the maturity or otherwise of candidates preparing for ordination. The maturity of the body of the faithful is passed over without a word. A shame really when so much admirable catechetical and adult educational work is being done to promote the human growth of all the faithful. The Code itself has an interesting section on the religious life. Its predecessor, the Code of 1917, had 4000 norms, the present Code has 700. Most of the disciplinary norms about confessors, dowries, enclosure and dismissal have been dropped. When I first opened the new Code I found myself turning up chapter four of the section on the religious life. It was entitled, 'The rights and duties of religious congregations and of their members'. I could not believe my eyes; I had *rights* . . . ! To confirm the truth of what I was reading I telephoned a friend, a Church historian, and casually checked out what I had been reading. 'Incidentally, did I have any rights in the Code of 1917?'

'Oh yes,' he answered. 'You had the right to be buried in consecrated ground.'

It gradually became clear to me that not only do I have rights, I actually have responsibilities too. I am responsible, in virtue of the obedience I have vowed, for the principles of spirituality, individuality, subsidiarity, co-responsibility and equality outlined by the Code. In plain English this means that I am as responsible as my congregation's legislators for ensuring that we avoid standardizing the religious life, that we ensure that a higher body never does what a lower body can do, that consultation be an integral part of decision-making and sexism be ruled out. This is a long way away from the sentimental portrait of religious obedience put out by films such as *The Nun's Story* and *The Sound of Music*, a long way away from Diderot's *La Religieuse* and its contemporary counterparts.

It sets up a serious conversation between people who vow religious obedience and people who are facing real live political and social choices in their own homes and workplaces. For we are both concerned with the same raw material, the same call from God to live creatively in the world of adult choices. It puts the same onus on us both and offers us both the same resources. For we are not called to make our decisions alone, nor to make them unaided. Each of us belongs to some sort of discerning community, some manifestation of Church which is intended to help us contextualize our truth and the tradition's truth. None of us is exonerated from the Christian task of knowing and naming God's call in our own world and our own times.

Afterword

❧❀❧

I cannot end this book with a conclusion. Of necessity I must end with an afterword because what I have been writing envisages the beginning of a conversation rather than its conclusion. My dedication read, 'I am glad we are not bishops'. Were I a bishop I would have different responsibilities, any teaching I did would have to come from a place which leans more heavily upon the past and speaks more concretely to the future. Of course a bishop can be prophetic — any Christian can be prophetic — but the unarmed, unprotected place from which I have been writing makes a good context for raising questions which both the religious life and lay life must increasingly address. I write from the 'interface of faith and experience with tradition', from the coal face of Christian living, and find myself wondering what kind of future faces us all. I write in the conviction that both lay life and religious life have a vision and both are for sharing.

The future

What profile of the religious life emerges from contemporary practice? What kind of future is likely or possible? Two possibilities are immediately evident. One is a return to past securities. Fundamentalism is alive and well, both to the right and to the left of present-day Christianity. The religious of the future could turn their back on the invitation to be human and holy people answering the one call we all receive at baptism with the appropriate answer they find within themselves and their own experience. They could withdraw to the underbelly of the Church's life, vanishing into obscurity as meaningless eschatological signs of an unknown and rather undesirable future kingdom. Alternatively, we can keep up the dialogue to which the Church

99

commits us by asking us to listen to the signs of the times. This dialogue is a conversation which enables us to look to the great richnesses of the tradition in an attempt to learn their lessons in our contemporary world and so to re-interpret both our understanding and our practice of the vows. If this book has enabled this exploration to gain some momentum, it will have fulfilled its brief.

If it has raised questions about the buzz words we use so blithely — 'mission' and 'community', for instance — it will also have served some purpose. If it has enabled lay people to use these words and the words chastity, poverty and obedience to describe what they know and find in their own experience then, I believe, something additional will have been achieved. For these words are part of the vocabulary Christians share in common and they gain in meaning when we use them to talk to each other. The language of the tradition is alive and well and crying out to find new expression in our midst. So too are the attitudes it encodes, about openness to God, about the conviction that this is God's world and that Christ is calling us still. We associate his call with the words spoken to his first disciples by the lakeside, 'Follow me' (Mark 1.18). This call was repeated at various stages in their lives and never more tellingly than when they had laboured through the night, apparently fruitlessly, he said to them, 'Put out into deep water' (Luke 5.4). Professed religious and lay people alike can take heart from these words, they are addressed to us all. The deep water is our common heritage and will reveal its secrets to all who seek to share their vision and bring its treasures into the light.

Books referred to in the text

❦

Bennett, Jo Anne Williams, *Downfall People*. Toronto: Seal Books 1987.

Byrne, Lavinia, *Mary Ward: A Pilgrim finds her Way*. Dublin: Avila Press 1984.

Chittister, Joan, OSB, *Women, Ministry and Church*. New York: Paulist Press 1983.

Fleming, David L., *The Spiritual Exercises of St Ignatius, A Literal Translation and Contemporary Reading*. St Louis: The Institute of Jesuit Sources.

Gilchrist, Roberta, 'The Spatial Archaeology of Gender Domains: a case study of Medieval English Nunneries', in the *Archaeological Review* from Cambridge, vol. 7, no. 1, Spring 1988. This forms the preliminary results of a thesis in progress at the University of York on 'The Archaeology of Female Piety: gender, ideology and material culture in late medieval England'.

Hebblethwaite, Margaret, *Finding God in All Things*. London: Collins 1987.

Hopkins, Gerard Manley, *Poems and Prose*. Selected and edited by W. H. Gardner. London: Penguin Books 1953.

Jantzen, Grace, *Julian of Norwich: Mystic and Theologian*. London: SPCK 1987.

Julian of Norwich, *Showings*. Classics of Western Spirituality. London: SPCK, New York: Paulist Press 1978.

Waal, Esther de, *Seeking God: The Way of St Benedict*. London: Collins 1984.

The Way, vol. 28, no. 4, October 1988.

Cowley Publications
is a work of the Society of St. John the
Evangelist, a religious community for
men in the Episcopal Church. The books
we publish are a significant part of our
ministry, together with the work of
preaching, spiritual direction, and
hospitality. Our aim is to provide books
that will enrich readers' religious
experience and challenge it with fresh
approaches to contemporary issues in
spirituality and theology.